BLACK & DECKER.

Stonework
& masonry projects

New Projects in Stone, Brick & Concrete

CREATIVE
PUBLISHING
international

MINNETONKA, MINNESOTA

Contents

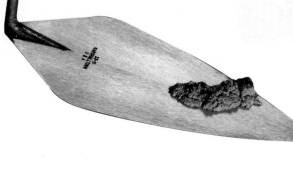

Executive Editor: Bryan Trandem
Creative Director: Tim Himsel
Managing Editor: Michelle Skudlarek
Editorial Director: Jerri Farris

Editors: Paul Currie, Jerri Farris, Daniel London, Phil Schmidt
Copy Editor: Jennifer Caliandro
Senior Art Director: Kevin Walton
Mac Designers: Kari Johnston, Jon Simpson
Technical Photo Editor: Keith Thompson
Technical Photo Assistants: Sean T. Doyle, Christopher Kennedy
Assisting Project Manager: Julie Caruso
Technical Reader: Lee Mosman
Photo Researcher: Angela Hartwell
Studio Services Manager: Marcia Chambers
Studio Services Coordinator: Carol Osterhus
Photo Team Leader: Chuck Nields
Photographers: Andrea Rugg, Rebecca Schmidt, Joel Schnell
Scene Shop Carpenters: Scott Ashfield, David O. Johnson,
　Greg Wallace, Dan Widerski
Director of Production Services: Kim Gerber
Production Manager: Helga Thielen

STONEWORK & MASONRY PROJECTS
Created by: The Editors of Creative Publishing international, Inc., in cooperation with Black & Decker. ●BLACK&DECKER. is a trademark of The Black & Decker Corporation and is used under license.

CREATIVE
PUBLISHING
international

Copyright © 2000
Creative Publishing international, Inc.
5900 Green Oak Drive
Minnetonka, Minnesota 55343
1-800-328-3895
All rights reserved

Printed on American Paper by:
R.R. Donnelly & Sons Co.
10 9 8 7 6 5 4 3 2 1

President/CEO: David D. Murphy
Vice President/Editor-in-Chief: Patricia K. Jacobsen
Vice President/Retail Sales & Marketing: Richard M. Miller

Masonry Projects

Library of Congress
Cataloging-in-Publication Data

Stonework and masonry projects: new
projects in stone, brick & concrete
p. cm. – (Black & Decker home
        improvement library)
Includes index.
ISBN 0-86573-582-4 (softcover)
ISBN 0-86573-468-2 (hardcover)
1. Stonemasonry—Amateurs' manuals. 2.
Masonry—Amateurs' manuals. 1. Title:
Stonework and masonry projects II. Cre-
ative Publishing international. III. Series.

TH5411 .S76 2001
693'.1–dc21
                    00-22691

Portions of *Stonework and Masonry Projects* are
taken from *The Complete Guide to Home Masonry,
Home Masonry Repairs & Projects, Landscape
Design & Construction, Building Garden Ornaments,
The Complete Photo Guide to Home Repair, Car-
pentry: Remodeling, Everyday Home Repairs,* and
Building Your Outdoor Home. Other titles from Cre-
ative Publishing international include:

*The New Everyday Home Repairs, Decorating
With Paint & Wallcovering, Carpentry: Tools •
Shelves • Walls • Doors, Basic Wiring & Electrical
Repairs, Workshop Tips & Techniques, Advanced
Home Wiring, Carpentry: Remodeling, Land-
scape Design & Construction, Bathroom Remod-
eling, Built-In Projects for the Home, Refinishing
& Finishing Wood, Exterior Home Repairs &
Improvements, Home Masonry Repairs & Pro-
jects, Building Porches & Patios, Flooring Pro-
jects & Techniques, Advanced Home Plumbing,
Remodeling Kitchens, The Complete Photo
Guide to Home Repair, The Complete Guide to
Home Plumbing, The Complete Guide to Home
Wiring, The Complete Guide to Decks, The
Complete Guide to Painting & Decorating.*

Introduction

Stone—the original masonry material—is indigenous to almost every part of the country, so the colors, textures and shapes of masonry materials naturally enhance any property. There are many reasons to include stone and other masonry materials in your landscape plans. Masonry structures can be designed to complement the style of virtually any home. Stone, brick and block structures can be solid or veneer; laid with or without mortar; straight, curved or angled; patterned or plain.

Although masonry materials have many natural advantages, it's important to assess them realistically: They are heavy and more difficult to cut and shape than either wood or plastic. And working with masonry requires patience, practice and attention to detail. However, if you're willing to invest the time and effort, you can produce top-quality projects at affordable prices. And along the way, you just may develop a love of the work and understandable pride in the results.

When you build with stone and other masonry materials, you're creating something that can be appreciated for generations. It's not unusual to see a building that has completely fallen to ruin except for masonry elements such as a stone chimney, a cement foundation, or perhaps a brick wall. This permanence can be a reason for caution as well as an advantage. If you're going to build with masonry, you need to do it right—the results of your efforts will be on display for a long, long time.

If a stone or masonry project—such as a wall, a pair of pillars or a garden path—is on your wish list, Stonework & Masonry Projects is the book for you. We developed it to help homeowners enjoy the satisfaction of building with stone and masonry. Some of the projects are challenging, but they all are realistic for do-it-yourselfers with time, energy and access to a small range of tools (having a few strong friends doesn't hurt, either).

Our goal is to help you learn the fundamentals of masonry construction so that you can work with just about any masonry material to add beauty and character to your home. We recommend that you start any project by consulting your local building inspector about the Building Code requirements in your area. Meeting these requirements will result in an attractive home improvement that will stand the test of time.

The "Introduction" helps you plan your projects and select tools and materials, so you can get the best results with the least effort.

Section two, "Masonry Techniques," discusses masonry materials—concrete, brick, block, stone, stucco, and more—and techniques that allow you to combine time-tested methods with a variety of masonry styles, from traditional to the latest trends.

Section three, "Masonry Projects," offers attractive designs and clear, concise plans that we've created with the do-it-yourselfer in mind. Some of these projects can be completed by yourself in just a few hours. For others, we recommend that you work with a group of friends and plan on spending a few days on the project.

The following pages are designed to help you design, plan, and complete projects in ways that help you get the best possible results. Before you pick up a trowel, read through the book, select projects that interest you, and look for similar structures in your community. Learn to identify what separates good masonry work from poor and to recognize what makes a masonry structure successful. With that understanding and the information in these pages, you'll be ready to construct projects that will be used and enjoyed for many years.

Test project layouts by using a rope or hose to outline proposed project areas. This will help you make decisions about size, scale, and shape. For curved walkways, use spacers between the borders of the project site to maintain an accurate, even width.

Planning & Designing Masonry Projects

Planning a masonry project begins with gathering ideas and envisioning the structure in place. The next step is to create a design that applies basic standards of masonry construction to produce a structurally sound project that complies with local Building Codes.

As you plan, it's important to consider size and scale, location, slope and drainage, reinforcement, material selection, and appearance requirements. By making detailed scaled drawings of the planned project, you can eliminate design flaws and accurately estimate building materials.

Bring home samples of the materials you have in mind and evaluate the way they blend with existing landscape elements. Many suppliers provide sample boards and sets of mortar tint to help you select complementary materials. As you select materials, consider the climate in your area. Deeply textured materials such as adobe and recycled brick are more suitable in regions where winter weather is mild—freezing temperatures compound the damaging effects of water. Local suppliers can point out materials that are appropriate to your region.

Tips for Designing a Masonry Project

Build a three-dimensional mock-up when planning a wall or other tall structure using tall stakes, mason's string, and landscape fabric, packing paper, or plastic. View the mock structure from all sides to get a sense of how it will obstruct views and access, and how it will blend with other landscape elements.

Test the drainage of your soil by digging a hole roughly 4" in diameter by 12" deep. Fill the hole with water and let it drain. If water remains after 24 hours, drainage is inadequate. When pouring a slab on such a site, lay plastic sheets along the base of the site to create a water barrier.

Common Masonry Projects Around the Home

Project	Level of Difficulty	Special Considerations
Decorative Accents (planters, birdbaths, home-made stepping stones, etc.)	Basic to Moderate	Good projects for beginners. Simple projects with few structural requirements. Most can be completed in a few hours.
Walkways & Paths	Basic to Moderate	Square corners are simple to create; curves and angles complicate the project. Walkways are subject to codes that govern size, reinforcement, location, and allowable materials. Often built adjacent to other permanent structures, creating a need for isolation joints.
Brick, Block & Stone Walls	Basic to Advanced	Simple garden-type walls are easy to build; project difficulty increases with size, complexity of stacking pattern, and need for reinforcement. Walls over 3 ft. tall generally require frost footings; wall caps or free-end pillars may be needed.
Driveways & Garage Floors	Advanced	Subbase preparation and grading are important and time-consuming. Can require special tools, such as a bull float, to handle large volume of concrete. High-strength concrete often required. Garage floors often steel-floated for a hard, semi-gloss surface.
Arches & Moon Windows	Advanced	Curved surfaces typically require more cutting of bricks or stones and a curved plywood form for construction. Special care is required to avoid strain or injury while positioning the materials.

Home centers carry the materials and tools you will need for most masonry projects. Many brick yards and stone suppliers also carry a wide range of specialty tools that can simplify your projects.

Estimating & Ordering Materials

Whether you are pouring a small slab or building an archway, estimate the dimensions of your project as accurately as possible. You will eliminate extra shopping trips and delivery costs.

Use the estimating chart (page 9) to determine how much of each masonry material you need. Since it is difficult to estimate these quantities exactly, add 10 percent to your estimate for each item. This will help you anticipate small oversights and allow for waste when cutting.

If you are building with brick, a local brick yard is where you'll find the best supply of bricklayer's materials. They can offer professional advice and often carry tools and other materials. The same goes for suppliers of natural stone.

Masonry tools, and materials such as concrete, mortar, and stucco mix, caulks, repair compounds, and metal fasteners, are available at home centers. However, you should consider the scale of your project before purchasing concrete or stucco by the bag. For large projects, such as a patio or driveway, you may want to hire a ready-mix supplier to deliver fresh concrete. Just remember, you will need a team of friends and plenty of tools on hand when the concrete arrives. With concrete and other troweled masonry, timing is critical.

How to Estimate Materials

Sand, gravel, topsoil (2" layer)	surface area (sq. ft.) ÷ 100 = tons needed
Standard brick pavers for walks and patios (4" × 8")	surface area (sq. ft.) × 5 = number of pavers needed
Standard bricks for walls and pillars (4" × 8")	surface area (sq. ft.) × 7 = number of bricks needed (single brick thickness)
Poured concrete (4" layer)	surface area (sq. ft.) × .012 = cubic yards needed
Flagstone	surface area (sq. ft.) ÷ 100 = tons of stone needed
Interlocking Block (6" × 16" face)	area of wall face (sq. ft.) × 1.5 = number of stones needed
Ashlar stone for 1-ft.-thick walls	area of wall face (sq. ft.) ÷ 15 = tons of stone needed
Rubble stone for 1-ft.-thick walls	area of wall face (sq. ft.) ÷ 35 = tons of stone needed
8" × 8" × 16" concrete block for freestanding walls	height of wall (ft.) × length of wall × 1.125 = number of blocks needed

Use this chart to estimate the materials you will need. Sizes and weights of materials may vary, so consult your supplier for more detailed information. The availability and cost of gravel and stone products vary from region to region. Visit a stone supplier to see the products firsthand. When sand, gravel, and other bulk materials are delivered, place them on a tarp to protect your yard. Make sure the tarp is as close to your work area as possible.

Local brick and stone suppliers will often help you design your project and advise you about estimating materials, local Building Codes, and climate considerations. Many suppliers offer a range of other services as well, such as coordinating landscapers and other contractors to work with you and offering classes in masonry construction.

Tools for mixing concrete and for site preparation include: a sturdy wheelbarrow (A) with a minimum capacity of 6 cubic ft.; power concrete mixer (B) for large poured concrete projects (more than ½-1 cubic yard); masonry hoe (C) and mortar box (D) for mixing mortar and small amounts of concrete; square-end spade (E) for removing sod by hand, excavating, and settling poured concrete; and tamper (F) for compacting the building site and subbase. Also shown: a sod cutter (G) for stripping sod for reuse.

Masonry Tools & Equipment

To work effectively with masonry products, you may need to buy or rent some special-purpose tools. Trowels, floats, edgers, and jointers are hand tools used to place, shape, and finish concrete and mortar. Chisels are used to cut and fit brick and block. Equip circular saws and power drills with blades and bits designed for use with masonry materials.

For most poured concrete projects, a power concrete mixer is a valuable tool. If the project requires more than one cubic yard of concrete, have pre-mixed concrete delivered to save time and back strain, while ensuring a uniform mixing consistency for the entire project. For small concrete or mortar-set projects, use a mortar box and masonry hoe.

Site preparation for large-scale projects can be simplified by the proper tools. It's economical to rent a power tamper, power sod cutter or power auger as required by your project. You may prefer to purchase smaller tools, such as a pick for excavating hard or rocky soil, a post-hole digger for digging a small number of holes, or a come-along for moving large rocks and other heavy objects without excessive lifting.

Make the layout process easier and more accurate by using the proper alignment and measuring tools, such as a framing square for setting project outlines, levels for setting forms and checking stacked masonry units, a story pole to calibrate stacked masonry units; a tape measure, line level, line blocks and mason's string, and a chalk line for making and marking layouts. Also make sure you have the necessary safety equipment on hand before you start your project, including gloves and protective eye wear.

Mason's tools include: a darby (A) for smoothing screeded concrete; mortar hawk (B) for holding mortar; pointing trowel (C) for tuck pointing stone mortar; wide pointing tool (D) for tuck pointing or placing mortar on brick and block walls; jointer (E) for finishing mortar joints; brick tongs (F) for carrying multiple bricks; narrow tuck-pointer (G) for tuck-pointing or placing mortar on brick and block walls; mason's trowel (H) for applying mortar; masonry chisels (I) for splitting brick, block, and stone; bullfloat (J) for float-ing large slabs; mason's hammers (K) for chipping brick and stone; maul (L) for driving stakes; square-end trowel (M) for concrete finishing; side edger (N) and step edger (O) for finishing inside and outside corners of concrete; joint chisel (P) for removing dry mortar; control jointer (Q) for creating control joints; tile nippers (R) for trimming tile; sled jointer (S) for smoothing long joints; steel trowel (T) for finishing concrete; magnesium or wood float (U) for floating concrete; screed board (V) for screeding concrete.

(continued next page)

Basic hand and power tools include: a shop broom (A) for keeping your work site clean and for creating a textured surface on poured concrete; bucket and scrub brush (B) for removing dirt and stains; stiff-bristle brushes (C) for cleaning tough stains and removing loose material; hand saw (D) for cutting forms; hacksaw (E) for trimming PVC pipe, rebar, and other materials; rubber mallet (F) for setting brick pavers; reciprocating saw (G) for cutting PVC, rebar, and other materials; crowbar (H) and pry bar (I) for rebuilding stone walls; pipe clamps (J) used when scoring large quantities of brick or block; aviation snips (K) for trimming metal ties and stucco lath; bolt cutters (L) for cutting rebar and wire mesh; circular saw (M) for scoring brick, block, and stone (using a masonry blade) or cutting wood forms (using a combination blade); hammer drill with masonry bit (N) for drilling into masonry; hammer (O) for driving nails into forms; power drill with masonry bit (P) for light drilling in masonry; caulk gun (Q) for sealing around fasteners and house trim; and garden hose with spray nozzle (R) for wetting masonry during curing and cleaning.

Working Safely

Working with masonry requires a variety of precautions to prevent injuries from caustic materials, sharp edges, flying shards of stone, and other materials:

• Wear a particle mask, gloves, and protective eye wear when handling or mixing dry mixes and when using striking or cutting tools such as mauls, chisels, and saws. Follow the manufacturer's safety precautions. Concrete and mortar mixes contain silica, which is hazardous in large quantities and will irritate skin.

• Wear a lifting belt for extra protection and use safe lifting techniques when moving masonry products, which tend to be quite heavy.

• Use a GFCI extension cord for plugging in power tools outdoors or when materials are wet. A GFCI cord protects against electrical shock caused by a faulty tool or a worn or wet cord or plug.

• Use scaffolding for projects that require extended time working at heights. When set up properly, scaffolding provides a much safer working platform than a ladder.

Wear protective equipment, including a particle mask, eye wear, and gloves when mixing masonry products. Concrete products can be health hazards, and they will irritate skin upon contact. Also wear a mask to protect yourself from dust when cutting concrete, brick, or block.

Tips for Working Safely

Wear a lifting belt to help prevent lower back strain when stacking brick and block, and when hand-mixing concrete products. Always lift with your legs, not your back, and keep the items being lifted as close to your body as you can.

Keep the job site clean and well organized by designating a tool area and by sweeping the work site frequently.

Masonry Techniques

Mixing & Throwing Mortar

Watching a professional brick-layer at work is an impressive sight, even for do-it-yourselfers who have completed numerous masonry projects successfully. The mortar practically flies off the trowel and seems to end up in perfect position to accept the next brick or block.

Although "throwing mortar" is an acquired skill that takes years to perfect, you can use the basic techniques successfully with just a little practice.

The first critical element to handling mortar effectively is the mixture. If it's too thick, it will fall off the trowel in a heap, not in the smooth line that is your goal. Add too much water and the mortar becomes messy and weak. Follow the manufacturer's directions, but keep in mind that the amount of water specified is an approximation. If you've never mixed mortar before, experiment with small amounts until you find a mixture that clings to the trowel just long enough for you to deliver a controlled, even line that holds its shape after settling. Note how much water you use in each batch, and record the best mixture.

Mix mortar for a large project in batches; on a hot, dry day a large batch will harden before you know it. If mortar begins to thicken, add water (called retempering); use retempered mortar within two hours.

Throwing mortar is a quick, smooth technique that requires practice. Load the trowel with mortar (page 18), then position the trowel a few inches above the starting point. In one motion, begin turning your wrist over and quickly move the trowel across the surface to spread mortar consistently. Proper mortar-throwing results in a rounded line about 2½" wide and about 2 ft. long.

Everything You Need:

Tools: Trowel, hoe, shovel.

Materials: Mortar mix, mortar box, plywood blocks.

Selecting the Right Mortar

Masonry mortar is a mixture of portland cement, sand, and water. Ingredients such as lime and gypsum are added to improve workability or control "setup" time. Every mortar mixture balances strength, workability, and other qualities. The strongest mortar is not always the best one for the job. A mortar that's too strong won't absorb stresses, such as those that occur as temperatures rise and fall. The result can be damage to masonry structures.

Each project and repair in this book includes a mortar mix recommendation. Always follow the guidelines for your project and the materials you've selected, and read the manufacturer's specifications on the mortar mix package. The chart below indicates the typical uses for the most commonly sold mortar mixes. Type N mortar mix is called for most often, because it offers a good blend of strength and workability.

Types of Mortar & Their Uses

Gone are the days when do-it-yourselfers had to mix mortar from scratch. These days, when you think of mortar, think of mortar mix, the standard term for the dry, prepackaged mixes available at home centers. For most of today's projects, simply select the proper mortar mixture, mix in water, and start to trowel. For some repair projects, adding a fortifier may be recommended. You can also tint your mortar to match your other materials.

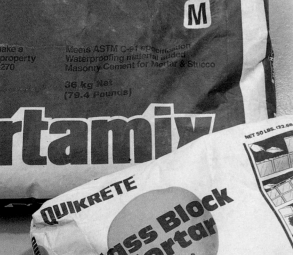

Type N
Medium-strength mortar for above grade outdoor use in non-load-bearing (freestanding) walls, barbecues, chimneys, soft stone masonry, and tuck-pointing.

Type S
High-strength mortar for exterior use at or below grade. Generally used in foundations, brick and block retaining walls, driveways, walks, and patios.

Type M
Very high-strength specialty mortar for load-bearing exterior stone walls, including stone retaining walls, and veneer applications.

Refractory Mortar
A calcium aluminate mortar that does not break down with exposure to high temperatures; used for mortaring around firebrick in fireplaces and barbecues. Chemical-set mortar is best, because it will cure even in wet conditions.

Glass Block Mortar
A specialty white type S mortar for glass block projects. Standard grey type S mortar is also acceptable for glass block projects.

17

How to Mix & Throw Mortar

1 Empty mortar mix into a mortar box and form a depression in the center. Add about ¾ of the recommended amount of water into the depression, then mix it in with a masonry hoe. Do not overwork the mortar. Continue adding small amounts of water and mixing until the mortar reaches the proper consistency. Do not mix too much mortar at one time—mortar is much easier to work with when it is fresh.

2 Set a piece of plywood on blocks at a convenient height, and place a shovelful of mortar onto the surface. Slice off a strip of mortar from the pile, using the edge of your mason's trowel. Slip the trowel point-first under the section of mortar and lift up.

3 Snap the trowel gently downward to dislodge excess mortar clinging to the edges. Position the trowel at the starting point, and "throw" a line of mortar onto the building surface (see technique photos, page 16). A good amount is enough to set three bricks. Do not get ahead of yourself. If you throw too much mortar, it will set before you are ready.

4 "Furrow" the mortar line by dragging the point of the trowel through the center of the mortar line in a slight back-and-forth motion. Furrowing helps distribute the mortar evenly.

Masonry fasteners include: J-bolt with nut and washers (A) for setting railings on fresh concrete; self-tapping coated steel screws (B) for hanging light-weight hardware on vertical surfaces; sleeve anchor (left) and wedge anchor (right) (C) for mounting gates and other heavy objects on vertical surfaces; lag screw expansion shield and screw (D) for mounting gates and other heavy objects; plastic anchor and wood screw (E) for light-duty mounting; removable T-anchor (F) for small diameter holes; expansion shield "flush anchor" and screw (G) for applications where the top of the fastener must be flush with the masonry surface; spring-loaded toggle bolt (H) for mounting in the void of a brick or block.

Working with Masonry Fasteners

Masonry fasteners allow you to mount hardware on masonry surfaces. The simplest and most effective method is to place the mounting hardware in fresh mortar or concrete. Start by making a sketch of the locations for the fasteners so you can set them as you build. Once the mortar or concrete sets, the hardware is secure.

When attaching a handrail to a freshly poured stoop, use hardware that attaches to a J-bolt. Embed the bolt so ¾" to 1" of it is exposed. Check for plumb and brace it in place for several minutes until the concrete firms up. Let the concrete cure for 24 hours before attaching the railing.

If you're installing hardware on an existing structure, mark locations for fasteners, then use a hammer drill with a carbide-tipped masonry bit

to drill holes. Or, for large posts, chip out holes with a maul and chisel. On horizontal surfaces, fill the hole with anchoring cement and place a J-bolt or other fastener in the cement. Hold or brace the fastener in place for several minutes until the cement begins to harden. Let the mortar cure for one week before installing gates or other heavy hardware. On vertical surfaces, use metal fasteners rated for the weight of the object you are hanging.

Mount fasteners on masonry veneer using a T-anchor or spring-loaded toggle bolt. Mark locations, then drill holes according to the fastener specifications, using a hammer drill and a carbide-tipped masonry bit. Once fasteners are in place, seal around them with masonry caulk. Let the mortar cure for one week before installing gates or other heavy hardware.

19

Poured concrete can be shaped and finished to create a wide variety of surfaces and structures around your home. In the photo above, the steps and the walkway blend together gracefully. The poured-concrete construction creates the impression that the two elements are a single unit.

Working with Concrete

Poured concrete is one of the most versatile and durable building materials available. You can use it to make just about any type of outdoor structure. Concrete costs less than other building materials, such as pressure-treated lumber or brick pavers. With a decorative finish such as exposed aggregate, or a tint added to the wet mixture, you can vary concrete's appearance.

Whether you're pouring one small footing or a whole driveway, timing and preparation are the most important factors in working with concrete. Poured concrete yields the most durable and attractive final finish when it is poured at an air temperature between 50° and 80°F and when

the finishing steps are completed carefully in the order described in this section.

Yet, concrete will harden to its final form whether you have finished working it or not. The best insurance policy against running out of time is thorough site preparation. Good preparation means fewer delays at critical moments, and leaves you free to focus on placing and smoothing the concrete—not on staking down loose forms or locating misplaced tools.

Stick to smaller-scale projects until you're comfortable working with concrete, and recruit helpers if you're taking on a large project.

Common Concrete Projects

A concrete walkway in a backyard or at a garage or side entrance is a good starter project. The techniques, even for angled walkways like the one shown above, are basic. Because no frost footing is required in most cases, and because walkways can be built to follow gradual slopes, little site preparation is needed. See "Pouring a Concrete Walkway" (pages 66 to 69).

A patio can be built and finished to blend well with the surrounding elements of just about any yard and house. Using permanent forms between sections allows the entire project to be treated as a series of smaller projects.

Garden steps can be built by making a series if concrete platforms framed with timbers. When finished with a non-skid surface, such as the exposed aggregate surface shown above, concrete steps offer a reliable walking surface. See "Building Garden Steps" (pages 72 to 79).

A poured concrete footing creates a sturdy base for poured concrete projects, as well as for projects built from brick or block. Requirements for footings are defined in your local Building Code. See "Pouring Footings" (pages 38 to 39).

Good site preparation is one of the keys to a successful project. Patience and attention to detail when excavating, building forms, and establishing a subbase help ensure that your finished project is level and stable and will last for many years.

Preparing the Project Site

The basic steps in preparing a project site are:

1) Laying out the project, using stakes and strings;

2) Clearing the project area and removing sod;

3) Excavating the site to allow for a subbase and footings (as needed) and concrete;

4) Laying a subbase for drainage and stability and pouring footings (as needed);

5) Building and installing reinforced wood forms.

Proper site preparation varies from project to project and site to site. Plan on a subbase of compactible gravel. Some projects require footings (pages 38 to 41) that extend past the frost line, while others, such as sidewalks, do not. Ask your local building inspector if you need metal reinforcement.

If your yard slopes more than 1" per ft., you may need to add or remove soil to level the surface; a landscape engineer or a building inspector can advise you on how to prepare your yard for your project.

SAFETY TIP: Beware of buried electric and gas lines when digging. Contact your local public utility company before you start digging.

Everything You Need:

Tools: Rope, carpenter's square, hand maul, tape measure, mason's string, line level, spade, sod cutter, straightedge, level, wheelbarrow, shovel, hand tamper, circular saw, drill.

Materials: 2 × 4 lumber, 3" screws, compactible gravel, vegetable oil or commercial release agent.

Tips for Preparing the Project Site

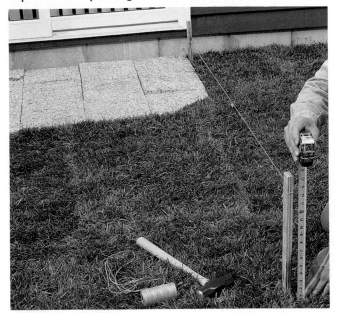

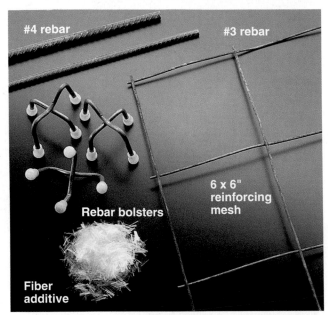

Measure the slope of the building site to determine if you need to do grading work before you start your project. First, drive stakes at each end of the project area. Attach a mason's string between the stakes and use a line level to set it at level. At each stake, measure from the string to the ground. The difference between the measurements (in inches) divided by the distance between stakes (in feet) will give you the slope (in inches per foot). If the slope is greater than 1" per foot, you may need to regrade the site.

Reinforcement materials: *Metal rebar,* available in sizes ranging from #2 (⅛" diameter) to #5 (⅝" diameter) is used to reinforce narrow concrete slabs, like sidewalks, and in masonry walls. For most projects, #3 rebar (⅜" diameter) is suitable. *Wire mesh* (sometimes called re-mesh) is most common in 6 × 6" grids. It is usually used for broad surfaces, like patios. *Bolsters* suspend rebar and wire mesh off the subbase. *Fiber additive* is mixed into concrete to strengthen small projects that receive little traffic.

Add a compactible gravel subbase to provide a level, stable foundation for the concrete. The compactible gravel also improves drainage—an important consideration if you are building on soil that is high in clay content. For most building projects, pour a layer of compactible gravel about 5" thick, and use a tamper to compress it to 4".

When pouring concrete next to structures, glue a ½"-thick piece of asphalt-impregnated fiber board to the adjoining structure to keep the concrete from bonding with the structure. The board creates an isolation joint, allowing the structures to move independently, minimizing the risk of damage.

How to Lay Out & Excavate a Building Site

1 Lay out a rough project outline with a rope or hose. Use a carpenter's square to set perpendicular lines. To create the actual layout, begin by driving wood stakes near each corner of the rough layout. The goal is to arrange the stakes so they are outside the actual project area, but in alignment with the borders of the project. Where possible, use two stakes set back 1 ft. from each corner, so strings intersect to mark each corner (below). NOTE: In projects built next to permanent structures, the structure will define one project side.

2 Connect the stakes with mason's strings. The strings should follow the actual project outlines. To make sure the strings are square, use the 3-4-5 triangle method: measure and mark points 3 ft. out from one corner along one string, and 4 ft. out along the intersecting string at the corner. Measure between the points, and adjust the positions of the strings until the distance between the points is exactly 5 ft. A helper will make this easier.

3 Reset the stakes, if necessary, to conform to the positions of the squared strings. Check all corners with the 3-4-5 method, and adjust until the entire project area is exactly square. This can be a lengthy process with plenty of trial and error, but it is very important to the success of the project, especially if you plan to build on the concrete surface.

4 Attach a line level to one of the mason's strings to use as a reference. Adjust the string up or down as necessary until it is level. Adjust the other strings until they are level, making sure that intersecting strings contact one another (this ensures that they are all at the same height relative to ground level).

5 Most concrete surfaces should have a slight slope to direct water runoff away from your house. To create a slope, shift the level mason's strings on opposite sides of the project downward on their stakes (the lower end should be farther away from the house). To create a standard slope of ⅛" per foot, multiply the distance between the stakes on one side (in feet) by ⅛. For example, if the stakes were 10 ft. apart, the result would be ¹⁰⁄₈ (1¼"). You would move the strings down 1¼" on the stakes on the low ends.

6 Start excavating by removing the sod. Use a sod cutter if you wish to reuse the sod elsewhere in your yard (lay the sod as soon as possible). Otherwise, use a square-end spade to cut away sod. Strip off the sod at least 6" beyond the mason's strings to make room for 2 × 4 forms. You may need to remove the strings temporarily for this step.

7 Make a story pole as a guide for excavating the site. First, measure down to ground level from the high end of a slope line. Add 7½" to that distance (4" for the subbase material and 3½" for the concrete if you are using 2 × 4 forms). Mark the total distance on the story pole, measuring from one end. Remove soil from the site with a spade. Use the story pole to make sure the bottom of the site is consistent (the same distance from the slope line at all points) as you dig. Check points at the center of the site using a straightedge and a level placed on top of the soil.

8 Lay a subbase for the project (unless your project requires a frost footing, pages 38 to 41). Pour a 5"-thick layer of compactible gravel in the project site, and tamp until the gravel is even and compressed to 4" in depth. NOTE: The subbase should extend at least 6" beyond the project outline.

1 A form is a frame, usually made from 2 × 4 lumber, laid around a project site to contain poured concrete and establish its thickness. Cut 2 × 4s to create a frame with inside dimensions equal to the total size of the project.

2 Use the mason's strings that outline the project as a reference for setting form boards in place. Starting with the longest form board, position the boards so the inside edges are directly below the strings.

3 Cut several pieces of 2 × 4 at least 12" long to use as stakes. Trim one end of each stake to a sharp point. Drive the stakes at 3-ft. intervals at the outside edges of the form boards, positioned to support any joints in the form boards.

4 Drive 3" deck screws through the stakes and into the form board one one side. Set a level so it spans the staked side of the form and the opposite form board, and use the level as a guide as you stake the second form board so it is level with the first (for large projects, use the mason's strings as the primary guide for setting the height of all form boards).

5 Once the forms are staked and leveled, drive 3" deck screws at the corners. Coat the insides of the forms with vegetable oil or a commercial release agent so concrete won't bond with them. TIP: Tack nails to the outsides of the forms to mark locations for control joints at intervals roughly 1½ times the slab's width (but no more than 30 times its thickness).

Variations for Building Forms

Use plywood (top left photo) for building taller forms for projects like concrete steps. Gang-cut plywood form sides, and brace with 2 × 4 arms attached to stakes and 2 × 4 cleats at the sides. **Use the earth as a form (bottom left photo)** when building footings for poured concrete building projects. Use standard wood forms for the tops of footings for building with brick or block, when the footing will be visible. **Create curves (right)** with ⅛" hardboard attached at the inside corners of a form frame. Drive support stakes behind the curved form.

Tips for Laying Metal Reinforcement

Cut metal rebar with a reciprocating saw that is equipped with a metal-cutting blade (cutting metal rebar with a hacksaw can take 5 to 10 minutes per cut). Use bolt cutters to cut wire mesh.

Overlap joints in metal rebar by at least 12", then bind the ends together with heavy-gauge wire. Overlap seams in wire mesh reinforcement by 12".

Leave at least 1" of clearance between the forms and the edges or ends of metal reinforcement. Use bolsters or small chunks of concrete to raise wire mesh reinforcement off the subbase, but make sure it is at least 2" below the tops of the forms.

Too dry

Too wet

Correct

Estimating & Mixing Concrete

If you are mixing concrete on-site, you can purchase the ingredients separately and blend them or purchase bags of pre-mixed concrete, and simply add water. For small do-it-your-self projects, premixed products are recommended. By following the instructions on the bag, you can achieve uniform results from one batch to the next. Never mix less than a full bag of mix, however, since key ingredients may have settled to the bottom.

For smaller projects, a wheel-barrow or mortar box makes a good mixing container. For larger projects, consider renting or buying a power mixer, or having the concrete delivered by a ready-mix company.

A good mixture is crucial to any successful concrete project. Properly mixed concrete is damp enough to form in your hand when you squeeze, and dry enough to hold its shape. If the mixture is too dry, the aggregate will be difficult to work, and will not smooth out easily to produce an even, finished appearance. A wet mixture will slide off the trowel, and may cause cracking and other defects in the finished surface.

Components of Concrete

The basic ingredients of concrete are the same, whether the concrete is mixed from scratch, purchased premixed, or delivered by a ready-mix company. Portland cement is the bonding agent. It contains crushed lime, cement, and other bonding minerals. Sand and a combination of aggregates add volume and strength to the mix. Water activates the cement, then evaporates, allowing the concrete to dry into a solid mass. By varying the ratios of the ingredients, professionals can create concrete with special properties that are suited for specific situations.

Premixed concrete products contain all the components of concrete. Just add water, mix, and pour. Usually sold in 60-lb. bags that yield roughly ½ cu. ft., these products include ingredients with specific properties for specific applications. General-purpose concrete mix (A) is usually the least expensive, and is suitable for most do-it-yourself, poured concrete projects. Fiber-reinforced concrete mix (B) contains strands of fiberglass that increase the strength of the concrete. If approved by your local building inspector, you can use fiber-reinforced concrete for some slabs, instead of general-purpose concrete, eliminating the need for metal reinforcement. High-early-strength premixed concrete (C) contains agents that cause it to set quickly—a desirable property if you are pouring in cool weather. Sand mix (D) contains no mixed aggregate, and is used only for surface repairs where larger aggregate is not desirable.

Tips for Estimating Concrete

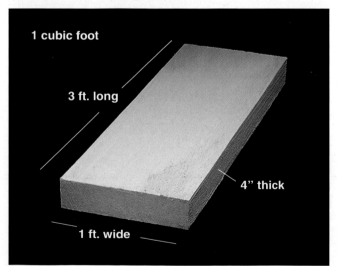

Concrete Coverage		
Volume	Thickness	Surface Coverage
1 cu. yd.	2"	160 sq. ft.
1 cu. yd.	3"	110 sq. ft.
1 cu. yd.	4"	80 sq. ft
1 cu. yd.	5"	65 sq. ft.
1 cu. yd.	6"	55 sq. ft.
1 cu. yd.	8"	40 sq. ft.

Measure the width and length of the project in feet, then multiply the dimensions to get the square footage. Measure the thickness in feet (4" thick equals ⅓ ft.), then multiply the square footage times the thickness to get the cubic footage. For example, 1 ft. × 3 ft. × ⅓ ft. = 1 cu. ft. Twenty-seven cubic feet equals one cubic yard.

Coverage rates for poured concrete are determined by the thickness of the slab. The same volume of concrete will yield less surface area if the thickness of the slab is increased. The chart above shows the relationship between slab thickness, surface area, and volume.

How to Mix Concrete by Hand

1 Empty premixed concrete bags into a mortar box or wheelbarrow. Form a hollow in the mound of dry mix, then pour water into the hollow. Start with one gallon of clean tap water per 60-lb. bag.

2 Work with a hoe, continuing to add water until a good consistency is achieved. Clear out any dry pockets from the corners. Do not overwork the mix. Also, keep track of how much water you use in the first batch so you will have a reliable recipe for subsequent batches.

How to Mix Concrete with a Power Mixer

1 Fill a bucket with 1 gallon of water for each 60-lb. bag of concrete you will use in the batch (for most power mixers, 3 bags is workable). Pour in half the water. Before you start power-mixing, review the operating instructions carefully.

2 Add all of the dry ingredients, then mix for one minute. Pour in water as needed until the proper consistency is achieved, and mix for three minutes. Pivot the mixing drum to empty the concrete into a wheelbarrow. Rinse out the drum immediately.

Have ready-mix concrete delivered for large projects. Prepare the site and build the forms, and try to have helpers on hand to help you place and tool the concrete when it arrives.

Ordering Ready-mix Concrete

For large concrete jobs (1 cubic yard or more), have ready-mix concrete delivered to your site. Although it is more expensive, it saves time. Seek referrals, and check your telephone directory under "Concrete" for ready-mix sources.

Tips for preparing for concrete delivery:

- Fully prepare the building site.

- Discuss your project with the experts at the ready-mix company. They will help you decide how much and what type of concrete you need. To help you determine your quantity needs, see the chart on page 9.

- Call the supplier the day before the scheduled pour to confirm the quantity and delivery time.

- Read the receipt you get from the driver. It will tell you at what time the concrete was mixed. Before you accept the concrete, make sure no more than 90 minutes has elapsed between the time it was mixed and the time it was delivered.

Prepare a clear delivery path to the project site, so when the truck rolls up you are ready to pour. Lay planks over the forms and subbase to make a roadway for the wheelbarrows or concrete hoppers. If you have an asphalt or concrete driveway that is cracking, have the truck park on the street to prevent further damage.

Placing Concrete

Placing concrete involves pouring it into forms, then leveling and smoothing it with special masonry tools. Once the surface is smooth and level, control joints are cut and the edges are rounded. Special attention to detail in these steps results in a professional appearance. NOTE: If you plan to add a special finish, read "Finishing & Curing Concrete" (pages 36 to 37) before you begin your project.

> **Everything You Need:**
>
> Tools: Wheelbarrow, hoe, spade, hammer, mason's trowel, float, groover, edger.
>
> Materials: Concrete, 2 × 4 lumber, mixing container, water container.

Start pouring concrete at the farthest point from the concrete source, and work your way back.

Tips for Pouring Concrete

Do not overload your wheelbarrow. Experiment with sand or dry mix to find a comfortable, controllable volume. This also helps you get a feel for how many wheelbarrow loads it will take to complete your project.

Lay planks over the forms to make a ramp for the wheelbarrow. Avoid disturbing the building site by using ramp supports. Make sure you have a flat, stable surface between the concrete source and the forms.

How to Place Concrete

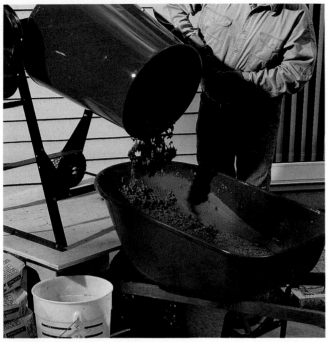

1 Load the wheelbarrow with fresh concrete. Make sure you have a clear path from the source to the site. Always load wheelbarrows from the front; loading wheelbarrows from the side can cause tipping.

2 Pour concrete in evenly spaced loads (each load is called a "pod"). Start at the end farthest from the concrete source, and pour so the top of the pod is a few inches above the top of the forms. Do not pour too close to the forms. NOTE: If you are using a ramp, stay clear of the end of the ramp.

3 Continue to place concrete pods next to preceding pods, working away from the first pod. Do not pour more concrete than you can tool at one time. Keep an eye on the concrete to make sure it does not harden before you can start tooling.

4 Distribute concrete evenly in the project area, using a masonry hoe. Work the concrete with a hoe until it is fairly flat, and the surface is slightly above the top of the forms. Remove excess concrete with a shovel.

(continued next page)

5 Immediately work the blade of a spade between the inside edges of the form and the concrete to remove trapped air bubbles that can weaken the concrete.

6 Rap the forms with a hammer or the blade of the shovel to help settle the concrete. This also draws finer aggregates in the concrete against the forms, creating a smoother surface on the sides. This is especially important when building steps.

7 Use a screed board—a straight piece of 2 × 4 long enough to rest on opposite forms—to remove the excess concrete before bleed water appears. Move the screed board in a sawing motion from left to right, and keep the screed flat as you work. If screeding leaves any valleys in the surface, add fresh concrete in the low areas and screed to level.

8 Cut control joints at marked locations with a mason's trowel, using a straight 2 × 4 as a guide. Control joints are designed to control where the slab cracks in the future, as natural heaving and settling occur. Without control joints, a slab may develop a jagged, disfiguring crack.

9 Wait until bleed water disappears (see box), then float in an arcing motion, with the leading edge of the tool up. Stop floating as soon as the surface is smooth.

Understanding Bleed Water

Timing is key to an attractive concrete finish. When concrete is poured, the heavy materials gradually sink, leaving a thin layer of water—known as *bleed water*—on the surface. To achieve an attractive finish, it's important to let bleed water dry before proceeding with other steps. Follow these rules to avoid problems:

- Settle and screed the concrete and add control joints (steps 5 through 8) immediately after pouring and before bleed water appears. Otherwise, crazing, spalling, and other flaws may develop.
- Let bleed water dry before floating or edging. Concrete should be hard enough that foot pressure leaves no more than a ¼"-deep impression.
- Do not overfloat the concrete; it may cause bleed water to reappear. Stop floating (step 9) if a sheen appears, and resume when it is gone.

NOTE: Bleed water does not appear with air-entrained concrete, which is used in regions where temperatures often fall below freezing.

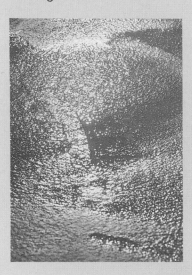

10 Once any bleed water has dried, draw a groover across the precut control joints (step 8), using a straight 2 × 4 as a guide. You may need to make several passes to create a smooth control joint.

11 Shape concrete with an edging tool between the forms and the concrete to create a smooth, finished appearance. You may need to make several passes. Use a wood float to smooth out any marks left by the groover or edger.

Exposed aggregate. Sometimes called "seeding," applying decorative aggregate to a fresh concrete surface creates an attractive effect with many design options. The photo above shows what various aggregates look like when they are used for an exposed-aggregate surface.

Broomed finish. Tool the concrete, then drag a broom across it. Wait until concrete is firm to the touch to achieve a finer texture and a more weather-resistant surface.

Finishing & Curing Concrete

Finishing and curing are critical final steps in a concrete project. They ensure that concrete reaches its maximum strength and remains free of defects that harm its appearance. There are many theories on the best way to cure concrete. In general, a good rule is to keep concrete damp and covered with plastic for at least a week.

A decorative finish dresses up concrete's appearance. Exposed-aggregate finishes are common on walkways and patios. Brooming (above) is a good option for improved traction. Stamping patterns is a popular way to create surfaces that imitate brick and other materials. Look around your neighborhood for other examples of creative finishes.

Everything You Need:

Tools: Broom, wheelbarrow, shovel, magnesium float, groover, edger, hose, coarse brush.
Materials: Plastic sheeting, "seeding" aggregate, water.

How to Cure Concrete

Keep concrete covered and damp for at least a week to maximize strength and to minimize surface defects. Lift the plastic occasionally and wet the surface so the concrete cures slowly.

How to Create an Exposed-aggregate Finish

1 After smoothing the surface with a screed board (step 7, page 34), let any bleed water disappear, then spread clean, washed aggregate evenly with a shovel or by hand. Spread smaller aggregate (up to 1" in diameter) in a single layer; for larger aggregate, maintain a separation between stones that is roughly equal to the size of one stone.

2 Pat the aggregate down with the screed board, then float the surface with a magnesium float until a thin layer of concrete covers the stones. Do not overfloat. If bleed water appears, stop floating and let it dry before completing the step. If you are seeding a large area, cover it with plastic to keep the concrete from hardening too quickly.

3 Cut control joints and tool the edges (step 8, page 34 and steps 10 to 11, page 35). Let concrete set for 30 to 60 minutes, then mist a section of the surface and scrub with a brush to remove the concrete covering the aggregate. If brushing dislodges some of the stones, reset them and try again later. When you can scrub without dislodging stones, mist and scrub the entire surface to expose the aggregate. Rinse clean. Do not let the concrete dry too long, or it will be difficult to scrub off.

4 After the concrete has cured for one week, remove the covering and rinse the surface with a hose. If a residue remains, try scrubbing it clean. If scrubbing is ineffective, wash the surface with a muriatic acid solution, then rinse immediately and thoroughly with water. OPTION: After three weeks, apply exposed-aggregate sealer.

Footings are required by Building Code for concrete, stone, brick, and block structures that adjoin other permanent structures or that exceed the height specified by local codes. *Frost footings* extend 8" to 12" below the frost line. *Slab footings*, which are typically 8" thick, may be recommended for low, freestanding structures built using mortar or poured concrete. Before starting your project, ask a building inspector about footing recommendations and requirements for your area.

Pouring Footings

Footings provide a stable, level base for brick, block, stone, and poured concrete structures. They distribute the weight of the structure evenly, prevent sinking, and keep structures from moving during seasonal freeze-thaw cycles.

The required depth of a footing is usually determined by the *frost line*, which varies by region. The frost line is the point nearest ground level where the soil does not freeze. In colder climates, it is likely to be 48" or deeper. Frost footings (footings designed to keep structures from moving during freezing temperatures) should extend 12" below the frost line for the area. Your local building inspector can tell you the frost line depth for your area.

Tips for Planning:

- Describe the proposed structure to your local building inspector to find out whether it requires a footing, and whether the footing needs reinforcement. In some cases, 8"-thick slab footings can be used, as long as the subbase provides plenty of drainage.

- Keep footings separate from adjoining structures by installing an isolation board.

- For smaller poured concrete projects, consider pouring the footing and the structure as one unit.

- A multi-wall project such as a barbecue may require a floating footing (page 121).

Options for Forming Footings

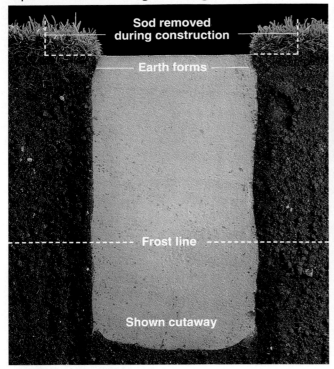

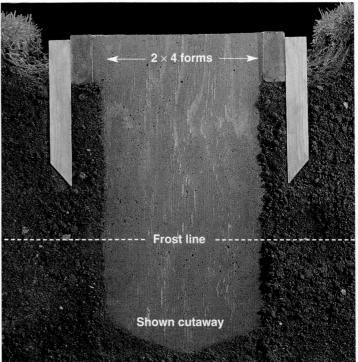

For poured concrete, use the earth as a form. Strip sod from around the project area, then strike off the concrete with a screed board resting on the earth at the edges of the top of the trench.

For brick, block, and stone, build level, recessed wood forms. Rest the screed board on the frames when you strike off the concrete to create a flat, even surface for stacking masonry units.

Tips for Building Footings

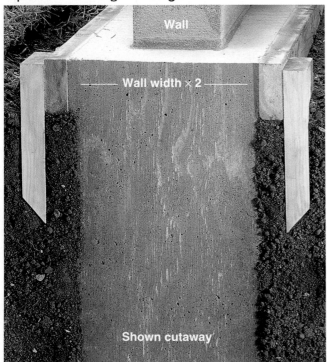

Make footings twice as wide as the wall or structure they will support. They also should extend at least 12" past the ends of the project area.

Add tie-rods if you will be pouring concrete over the footing. After the concrete sets up, press 12" sections of rebar 6" into the concrete. The tie-rods will anchor the footing to the structure it supports.

How to Pour a Footing

1 Make a rough outline of the footing, using a rope or hose. Outline the project area with stakes and mason's string.

2 Strip away sod 6" outside the project area on all sides, then excavate the trench for the footing to a depth 12" below the frost line.

3 Build and install a 2 × 4 form frame for the footing, aligning it with the mason's strings (page 26). Stake the form in place, and adjust to level.

VARIATION: If your project abuts another structure, such as a house foundation, slip a piece of fiber board into the trench to create an isolation joint between the footing and the structure (page 23). Use a few dabs of construction adhesive to hold it in place.

4 Make two #3 rebar grids to reinforce the footing. For each grid, cut two pieces of #3 rebar 8" shorter than the length of the footing, and two pieces 4" shorter than the depth of the footing. Bind the pieces together with 16-gauge wire, forming a rectangle. Set the rebar grids upright in the trench, leaving 4" of space between the grids and the walls of the trench. Coat the inside edge of the form with vegetable oil or commerical release agent.

5 Mix and pour concrete, so it reaches the tops of the forms (pages 32 to 35). Screed the surface, using a 2 × 4. Add tie-rods if needed (page 39). Float the concrete until it is smooth and level.

6 Cure the concrete for one week before you build on the footing. Remove the forms and backfill around the edges of the footing.

41

Working with stone demands patience and exacting attention to detail. But the rewards are many. Few masonry materials rival stone for spectacular beauty or durability. Consult the section on footings (38 to 41) for general guidance on pouring a footing suitable for your project.

Working with Stone

Building with stone is an enormously satisfying activity for anyone who enjoys developing a craft and doesn't mind hard work. Many issues affecting the ultimate look of your wall, pillar, arch, walk, or other stone project are entirely up to you to decide: Stone masons often prefer to recess the mortar in the joints so the stones—not the mortar—are emphasized. However, you may want to emphasize an attractively tinted mortar by adding extra mortar to the joints. Learn how to use mortar (pages 16 to 18) to create the effect you desire. You can also be creative in the way you "dress" stones for your project, chiseling the faces smooth, or letting them retain their natural look (pages 46 to 49). The following pages show you how to combine age-old techniques with state-of-the-art tools and materials to get the most satisfying results out of your stone work.

Wear a lifting belt to support your back and stomach muscles, and always bend at the knees as you lift stone. If you can't, the stone is too heavy to lift alone. Find a helper, and consider using an alternative technique for moving the stone into position.

Tips for Working with Stone

Stone work is a labor-intensive craft. Completing a big stone project on your own can take many days. Assemble a team for your project, rotating the responsibilities to keep everyone involved. With five or more working, you can complete many stone projects in a weekend.

Stone weighs 165 lb./cu. ft., on average. This can make it difficult to place stones precisely. There are many good techniques for moving stone safely and effectively. Use ramps and simple lifting or towing devices, such as chains, to simplify the task any time a stone is too heavy to lift comfortably.

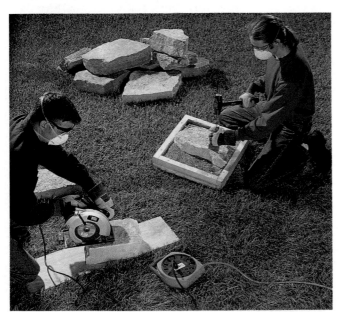

Cutting stones to fit is an important part of working with stone (pages 46 to 49). Keep a circular saw equipped with a silicon-carbide masonry blade on hand, along with a maul and chisel. Some stone masons prefer to do all their cutting with a maul and chisel to avoid unnaturally straight lines, but if there's a lot of splitting to do, you may want one person to take the first pass with a saw (called scoring) while another does the final splitting with a maul and chisel.

Organize stones by size and shape before starting your project. Taking the extra time required at the start of a project will save a lot of effort in the long run. If you're building a wall, stack long stones that will serve as tie stones (pages 50 to 51) in one area; filler, or wedge, stones in another area; and the remaining stones in a third.

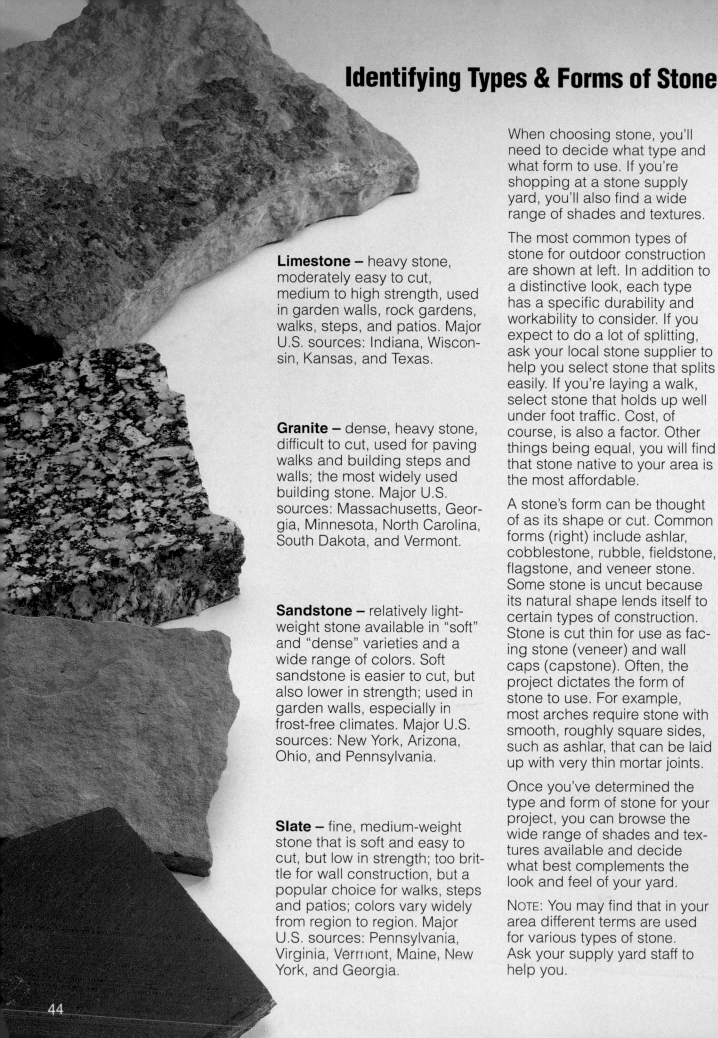

Identifying Types & Forms of Stone

When choosing stone, you'll need to decide what type and what form to use. If you're shopping at a stone supply yard, you'll also find a wide range of shades and textures.

The most common types of stone for outdoor construction are shown at left. In addition to a distinctive look, each type has a specific durability and workability to consider. If you expect to do a lot of splitting, ask your local stone supplier to help you select stone that splits easily. If you're laying a walk, select stone that holds up well under foot traffic. Cost, of course, is also a factor. Other things being equal, you will find that stone native to your area is the most affordable.

A stone's form can be thought of as its shape or cut. Common forms (right) include ashlar, cobblestone, rubble, fieldstone, flagstone, and veneer stone. Some stone is uncut because its natural shape lends itself to certain types of construction. Stone is cut thin for use as facing stone (veneer) and wall caps (capstone). Often, the project dictates the form of stone to use. For example, most arches require stone with smooth, roughly square sides, such as ashlar, that can be laid up with very thin mortar joints.

Once you've determined the type and form of stone for your project, you can browse the wide range of shades and textures available and decide what best complements the look and feel of your yard.

NOTE: You may find that in your area different terms are used for various types of stone. Ask your supply yard staff to help you.

Limestone – heavy stone, moderately easy to cut, medium to high strength, used in garden walls, rock gardens, walks, steps, and patios. Major U.S. sources: Indiana, Wisconsin, Kansas, and Texas.

Granite – dense, heavy stone, difficult to cut, used for paving walks and building steps and walls; the most widely used building stone. Major U.S. sources: Massachusetts, Georgia, Minnesota, North Carolina, South Dakota, and Vermont.

Sandstone – relatively lightweight stone available in "soft" and "dense" varieties and a wide range of colors. Soft sandstone is easier to cut, but also lower in strength; used in garden walls, especially in frost-free climates. Major U.S. sources: New York, Arizona, Ohio, and Pennsylvania.

Slate – fine, medium-weight stone that is soft and easy to cut, but low in strength; too brittle for wall construction, but a popular choice for walks, steps and patios; colors vary widely from region to region. Major U.S. sources: Pennsylvania, Virginia, Vermont, Maine, New York, and Georgia.

Flagstone – large slabs of quarried stone cut into pieces up to 3" thick; used in walks, steps, and patios. Pieces smaller than 16" sq. are often called *steppers*.

Split fieldstone

Fieldstone – stone gathered from fields, dry river beds, and hillsides; used in wall construction. When split into smaller, more manageable shapes, fieldstone is often used in mortared construction. Called *river rock* by some quarries because of the river-bed origin of some fieldstone.

Rubble – irregular pieces of quarried stone, usually with one split or finished face; widely used in wall construction.

Ashlar – quarried stone smooth-cut into large blocks ideal for creating clean lines with thin mortar joints.

Veneer stone – pieces of natural or manufactured stone, cut or molded for use in non-load-bearing, cosmetic applications, such as facing exterior walls or freestanding concrete block walls.

Cobblestone – small cuts of quarried stone or fieldstone; used in walks and paths.

Cutting & Shaping Stone

You can cut most stone by placing it directly on a bed of flat, soft ground, such as grass or sand, that will absorb some of the shock when the maul strikes the chisel. Use a sandbag for additional support. You can also build a simple cutting platform, called a *banker*, to support stones in a bed of sand. Protect yourself by wearing safety glasses and heavy gloves and using the proper tools for the job. A standard brickset chisel and hammer are too light for shaping stone and a carpenter's framing hammer is too light and its brittle material may chip when striking a chisel. The best tools are a pitching chisel for long, clean cuts, a pointing chisel for removing small bumps, a basic stone chisel, and a maul for tapping the chisels. A mason's hammer—with its pick at one end—is also useful for breaking off small chips.

It is often helpful to mark a stone for cutting while it sits in place on a wall or other structure, but never cut a stone while it is in place, even to remove a small bump. You risk splitting surrounding stones and breaking the mortar bond, if you're using mortar. For splitting, move the stone to soft ground or a banker at the base of the wall.

Everything You Need:

Tools: Maul, stone chisel, pitching chisel, pointing chisel, mason's hammer, circular saw, silicon-carbide masonry blades, GFCI extension cord.

Materials: Stone, sand, 2 × 2s, wallboard.

Tips for Cutting Stone

Laying stones works best when the sides (including the top and bottom) are roughly square. If a side is sharply skewed, score and split it with a pitching chisel, and chip off smaller peaks with a pointing chisel or mason's hammer. REMEMBER: a stone should sit flat on its bottom or top side without much rocking.

"Dress" a stone, using a pointing chisel and maul, to remove jagged edges or undesirable bumps. Position the chisel at a 30 to 45° angle at the base of the piece to be removed. Tap lightly all around the break line, then more forcefully, to chip off the piece. Position the chisel carefully before each blow with the maul.

Build a banker if you plan to do a lot of splitting. This simple sand-bed table provides a sturdy, but shock-absorbent work surface. Place it atop two columns of concrete block if you prefer to stand while splitting. Construct frames out of 2 × 2s, and sandwich a piece of ¾" plywood between the frames. Attach pieces by driving 3½" coarse-threaded wallboard screws through from both sides, and fill it with sand.

Grind the head of a chisel smooth on a grindstone any time the head begins to *mushroom* (curled edges appear). The curling results from repeated blows to the chisel with a maul. Small shards of metal can break free, becoming dangerous projectiles. REMEMBER: Always wear safety goggles when handling cutting tools.

Tips for Cutting Stone with a Circular Saw

A circular saw lets you precut the broad surfaces of stone with greater control and accuracy than most people can achieve with a chisel. It's a noisy process, so wear ear plugs, along with a dust mask and safety goggles. Install a toothless masonry blade on your saw and start out with the blade set to cut ⅛" deep. (Make sure the blade is designed for the material you're cutting. Some masonry blades are designed for hard materials like concrete, marble, and granite. Others are for soft materials, like concrete block, brick, flagstone, and limestone.) Wet the stone before cutting to help control dust, then make three passes, setting the blade ⅛" deeper with each pass. Repeat the process on the other side. A thin piece of wood under the saw protects the saw foot from rough masonry surfaces. REMEMBER: Always use a GFCI outlet or extension cord when using power tools outdoors.

How to Cut Fieldstone

1 Place the stone on a banker, or prop it with sandbags, and mark with chalk or a crayon all the way around the stone, indicating where you want it to split. If possible, use the natural fissures in the stone as cutting lines.

2 Score along the line using moderate blows with a chisel and maul, then strike solidly along the score line with a pitching chisel to split the stone. Dress the stone with a pointing chisel.

How to Cut Flagstone

1 Trying to split a large flagstone in half can lead to many unpredicted breaks. For best results, chip off small sections at a time. Mark the stone on both sides with chalk or a crayon, indicating where you want it to split. If there is a fissure nearby, mark your line there since that is probably where the stone will break naturally.

2 Score along the line on the back side of the stone (the side that won't be exposed) by moving a chisel along the line and striking it with moderate blows with a maul. OPTION: If you have a lot of cutting to do, reduce hammering fatigue by using a circular saw to score the stones, and a maul and chisel to split them. Keep the stone wet during cutting with a circular saw to reduce dust.

3 Turn the stone over, place a pipe or 2 × 4 directly under the chalk line, then strike forcefully with the maul on the end of the portion to be removed.

OPTION: If a paving stone looks too big compared to other stones in your path, simply set the stone in place and strike a heavy blow to the center with a sledge hammer. It should break into several usable pieces.

Laying Stone

Natural stone is heavy material—about 165 lb./cubic foot on average. So, the first thing to remember when laying stone is to handle it with care so you avoid injury to yourself and others. The methods of laying stone are as varied as the stone masons who practice the craft. But all of them would agree on a few general principles:

- Thinner joints are stronger joints. Whether you are using mortar or dry-laying stone, the more contact between stones, the more resistance to any one stone dislodging.

- *Tie stones* are essential in vertical structures, such as walls or pillars. These long stones span at least two-thirds the width of the structure, tying together the shorter stones around them.

- When working with mortar, most stone masons point their joints deep for aesthetic reasons. The less mortar is visible, the more the stone itself is emphasized.

- Long vertical joints, or *head* joints, are weak spots in a wall. Close the vertical joints by overlapping them with stones in the next course, similar to a running bond pattern in a brick or block wall.

- The sides of a stone wall should have an inward slope (called *batter*) for maximum strength. This is especially important with dry-laid stone. Mortared walls require less batter.

Keep mortar joints thin—thin joints are the strongest. When working with mortar, joints should be ½ to 1" thick. Mortar is not intended to create gaps between stones, but to fill the inevitable gaps and strengthen the bonds between stones. Wiggle a stone once it is in place to get it as close as possible to adjoining stones.

Blend large and small stones in walks or in vertical structures to achieve the most natural appearance. In addition to enhancing visual appeal, long stones in a walk act like the tie stones in a wall, adding strength by bonding with other stones.

Place uneven stone surfaces down and dig out the soil underneath until the stone lies flat. Use the same approach in the bottom course of a dry-laid wall, only make sure stones at the base of a wall slope toward the center of the trench.

Tips for Laying Stone in Walls & Other Structures

Tie stones are long stones that span most of the width of a wall, tying together the shorter stones, and increasing the wall's strength. As a guide, figure that 20 percent of the stones in a structure should be tie stones.

A shiner is the opposite of a tie stone—a flat stone on the side of a wall that contributes little in terms of strength. A shiner may be necessary when no other stone will fit in a space. Use shiners as seldom as possible, and use tie stones nearby to compensate.

Lay stones in horizontal courses, where possible, a technique called *ashlar* construction. If necessary, stack two to three thin stones to match the thickness of adjoining stones.

With irregular stone, such as untrimmed rubble or field stone, building course by course is difficult. Instead, place stones as needed to fill gaps and to overlap the vertical joints.

Use a batter gauge and level to lay up dry stone structures so the sides slope inward. Slope the sides of a wall 1" for every 2 ft. of height—less for ashlar and free-standing walls, twice as much for round stone and retaining walls.

Common types of brick and block used for residential construction include: decorative block (A) available colored or plain, decorative concrete pavers (B), fire brick (C), standard 8 × 8 × 16" concrete block (D), half block (E), combination corner block (F), queen-sized brick (G), standard brick pavers (H), standard building bricks (I), and limestone wall cap (J).

Working with Brick & Block

The first step in building a patio, wall, or other brick or block project is to identify a suitable construction method and practice the techniques you'll use along the way. If you are building a wall or covering an old concrete slab with brick or brick pavers, you'll need to use wet mortar to create a strong bond. The sand-set and dry mortar techniques are suitable for patios and driveways, where sand or dry mortar is enough to hold the bricks firmly in place. Most block walls are built with wet mortar, but an attractive garden wall is easily built by dry-laying blocks and coating them with surface bonding cement.

In addition to settling on a construction method, you need to select a style (above) and pattern to match your tastes and the construction method. Standard bricks can be arranged in several patterns, including: *running bond* and *stack bond.* Stack bond is not as strong as running bond; re-

inforcement typically is required. Use the chart on page 9 to estimate how many bricks or blocks you'll need.

Test project layouts using ⅜" spacers between masonry units to make sure the planned dimensions work. Create a plan that uses whole brick or blocks to the greatest extent possible, reducing the amount of cutting required.

Keep structures as low as you can. Local codes require frost footings and additional reinforcement for permanent walls or structures that exceed maximum height restrictions. You can often simplify your project by designing walls that are below those restrictions. If you want greater privacy without raising the height of a wall, add a lattice panel or other decorative element to the top of masonry walls.

Tips for Planning a Brick or Block Project

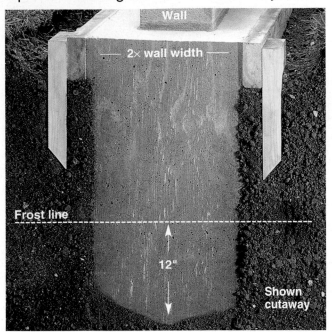

Build a frost footings if a structure is more than 2 ft. tall or if it is tied to another permanent structure. Frost footings should be twice as wide as the structure they support and should extend 8" to 12" below the frost line (pages 38 to 41).

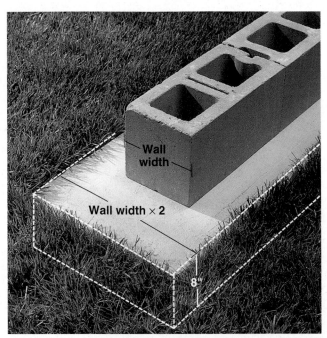

Pour a reinforced concrete slab for brick, block, stone, or poured concrete structures that are free-standing and under 2 ft. tall. The slab should be twice the wall's width, flush with ground level, and at least 8" thick. Ask your building inspector about local requirements. Slabs are poured using the techniques for pouring a walkway (pages 66 to 69).

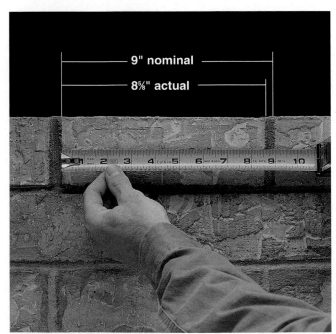

Do not add mortar joint thickness to total project dimensions when planning brick and block projects. The actual sizes of bricks and blocks are ⅜" smaller than the nominal size to allow for ⅜"-wide mortar joints. For example, a 9" (nominal) brick has an actual dimension of 8⅝", so a wall that is built with four 9" bricks and ⅜" mortar joints will have a finished length of 36" (4 × 9").

Test the water absorption rate of bricks to determine their density. Squeeze out 20 drops of water in the same spot on the surface of a brick. If the surface is completely dry after 60 seconds, dampen the bricks with water before you lay them to prevent them from absorbing moisture from the mortar before it has a chance to set.

How to Cut Brick

Score all four sides of the brick first with a brickset chisel and maul when cuts fall over the web area, and not over the core. Tap the chisel to leave scored cutting marks ⅛" to ¼" deep, then strike a firm final blow to the chisel to split the brick. Properly scored bricks split cleanly with one firm blow.

OPTION: When you need to split a lot of bricks uniformly and quickly, use a circular saw fitted with a masonry blade to score the bricks, then split them individually with a chisel. For quick scoring, clamp the bricks securely at each end with a pipe or bar clamp, making sure the ends are aligned. REMEMBER: Wear eye protection when using striking or cutting tools.

OPTION: A brick splitter makes accurate, consistent cuts in bricks and pavers with no scoring required. It is a good idea to rent one if your project requires many cuts. To use the brick splitter, first mark a cutting line on the brick, then set the brick on the table of the splitter, aligning the cutting line with the cutting blade on the tool.

How to Cut Concrete Block

1 Mark cutting lines on both faces of the block, then score ⅛" to ¼"-deep cuts along the lines, using a circular saw equipped with a masonry blade.

2 Use a mason's chisel and maul to split one face of the block along the cutting line. Turn the block over and split the other face.

OPTION: Cut half blocks from combination corner blocks. Corner blocks have preformed cores in the center of the web. Score lightly above the core, then rap with a mason's chisel to break off half blocks.

Laying Brick & Block

Patience, care, and good technique are the key elements to building brick structures that have a professional look. Start with a sturdy, level footing, and don't worry if your initial attempts aren't perfect. Survey your work often and stop when you spot a problem. As long as the mortar's still soft, you can remove units and try again.

The first project, building a double-wythe brick wall, features one method of construction: laying up the ends of the wall first, then filling in the interior bricks. The alternate method, laying one course at a time, is shown with concrete block.

Everything You Need:

Tools: Gloves, trowel, chalk line, level, line blocks, mason's string, jointing tool.

Materials: Mortar, brick, wall ties, rebar (optional).

Buttering is a term used to describe the process of applying mortar to the end of a brick or block before adding it to the structure being built. Apply a heavy layer of mortar to one end of a brick, then cut off the excess with a trowel.

How to Build a Double-wythe Brick Wall

1 Dry-lay the first course by setting down two parallel rows of brick, spaced ¾" to 1" apart. Use a chalk line to outline the location of the wall on the slab. Draw pencil lines on the slab to mark the ends of the bricks. Test-fit the spacing with a ⅜"-diameter dowel, then mark the locations of the joint gaps to use as a reference after the spacers are removed.

2 Dampen the concrete slab or footing with water, and dampen the bricks or blocks if necessary (page 53). Mix mortar and throw a layer of mortar on the footing for the first two bricks of one wythe at one end of the layout. Butter the inside end of the first brick, then press the brick into the mortar, creating a ⅜" mortar bed. Cut away excess mortar.

(continued next page)

Metal wall tie

11 Lay the remaining field bricks. The last brick, called the closure brick, should be buttered at both ends. Center the closure brick between the two adjoining bricks, then set in place with the trowel handle. Fill in the first three courses of each wythe, moving the mason's string up one course after completing each course.

12 In the fourth course, set metal wall ties into the mortar bed of one wythe and on top of the brick adjacent to it. Space the ties 2 to 3 ft. apart, every three courses. For added strength, set metal rebar into the cavities between the wythes and fill with thin mortar.

13 Lay the remaining courses, installing metal ties every third course. Check with mason's string frequently for alignment, and use a level to make sure the wall is plumb and level.

14 Lay a furrowed mortar bed on the top course, and place a wall cap on top of the wall to cover empty spaces and provide a finished appearance. Remove any excess mortar. Make sure the cap blocks are aligned and level. Fill the joints between cap blocks with mortar.

How to Lay Concrete Block

1 Draw reference lines and throw a mortar bed (page 55). Set a combination corner block and press it into the mortar to create a ⅜"-thick bed joint. Hold the block in place and cut away the excess mortar (save the excess for the next section of the mortar bed). Use a level to make sure the block is level and plumb. Make any necessary adjustments by rapping on the high side with the handle of a trowel. Be careful not to displace too much mortar.

2 Drive a stake at each end of the project and attach one end of a mason's string to each stake. Thread a line level onto the string and adjust the string until it is level and flush with the top of the corner block. Throw a mortar bed and set a corner block at the other end. Adjust the block so it is plumb and level, making sure it is aligned with the mason's string.

3 Throw a mortar bed for the second block at one end of the project: butter one end of a standard block and set it next to the corner block, pressing the two blocks together so the joint between them is ⅜" thick. Tap the block with the handle of a trowel to set it, and adjust the block until it is even with the mason's string. Be careful to maintain the ⅜" joint.

4 Install all but the last block in the first course, working from the ends toward the middle. Align the blocks with the mason's string. Clean excess mortar from the base before it hardens.

(continued next page)

5 Butter the flanges on both ends of a standard block for use as the "closure block" in the course. Slide the closure block into the gap between blocks, keeping the mortar joints an even thickness on each side. Align the block with the mason's string.

6 Apply a 1"-thick mortar bed for the half block at one end of the wall, then begin the second course with a half block.

7 Set the half block into the mortar bed with the smooth surfaces facing out. Use the level to make sure the half block is plumb with the first corner block, then check to make sure it is level. Adjust as needed. Install a half block at the other end.

Vertical joints

VARIATION: If your wall has a corner, begin the second course with a full-sized end block that spans the vertical joint formed where the two walls meet. This layout creates and maintains a running bond for the wall.

8 Attach a mason's string for reference, securing it either with line blocks or a nail. If you do not have line blocks, insert a nail into the wet mortar at each end of the wall, then wind the mason's string around and up to the top corner of the second course, as shown above. Connect both ends and draw the mason's string taut. Throw a mortar bed for the next block, then fill out the second course, using the mason's string as a reference line.

9 Every half-hour, tool the fresh mortar joints with a jointing tool and remove any excess mortar. Tool the horizontal joints first, then the vertical joints. Cut off excess mortar, using a trowel blade. When the mortar has set, but is not too hard, brush any excess mortar from the block faces. Continue building the wall until it is complete.

OPTION: When building stack bond walls with vertical joints that are in alignment, use wire reinforcing strips in the mortar beds every third course (or as required by local codes) to increase the strength of the wall. The wire should be completely embedded in the mortar.

10 Install a wall cap on top of the wall to cover the empty spaces and create a finished appearance. Set the cap pieces into mortar beds, then butter an end with mortar. Level the cap, then tool to match the joints in the rest of the wall.

Masonry Projects

Flagstone walkways combine charm with durability and work well in casual or formal settings. Flagstone is also a popular material for patios, and can be set in sand (pages 70 to 71) or mortared in place. TIP: Prevent damage to the edging material by trimming near the walkway with a line-feed trimmer instead of a mower.

Walks, Paths & Steps

Walkways and paths serve as "hallways" between heavily used areas of your yard and entryways to your home. They can be used to direct traffic or to guide you toward a favorite landscape feature, such as a pond or flower bed. They can also create a visual corridor that directs the eye from one area to another.

Curved paths have a softer, more relaxed effect. Straight or angular routes fit well in contemporary landscape designs.

Garden paths often are made from loose materials, such as crushed rock, held in place by edging. Walkways are more durable when made from stone or brick paving materials set in sand

or mortar. Poured concrete sidewalks are practical and extremely durable. Most paving techniques used in patio construction can be used for walkways as well.

A frost footing is not required under walk, paths, or steps, but you will need to remove sod and excavate the site for most projects. The depth of the excavation varies from project to project and depends on the thickness of the masonry material, plus the thickness of the sand or compactible gravel subbase. The subbase provides a more stable surface than the soil itself and an opportunity for water to run off so it does not pool directly under the masonry.

Tips for Building a Walkway

Use a sod cutter to strip grass from your pathway site. Available at most rental centers, sod cutters excavate to a very even depth. The cut sod can be replanted in other parts of your lawn.

Install stakes and strings when laying out straight walkways, and measure from the strings to ensure straight sides and uniform excavation depth.

Options for Directing Water off Walkways

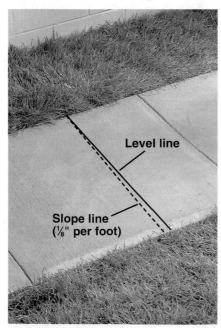

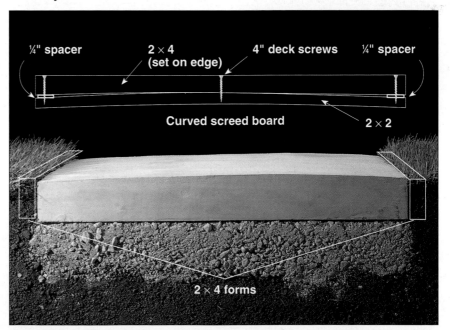

Slope walkways away from the house to prevent water damage to the foundation or basement. Outline the location of the walkway with level mason's strings, then lower the outer string to create a slope of ⅛" per foot (see page 24).

Crown the walkway so it is ¼" higher at the center than at the edges. This will prevent water from pooling on the surface. To make the crown, construct a curved screed board by cutting a 2 × 2 and a 2 × 4 long enough to rest on the walkway forms. Butt them together edge to edge and insert a ¼" spacer between them at each end. Attach the parts with 4" deck screws driven at the center and the edges. The 2 × 2 will be drawn up at the center, creating a curved edge. Screed the concrete with the curved edge of the screed board facing down.

Pouring a Concrete Walkway

Pouring a concrete walkway is one of the most practical projects you can master as a homeowner. Once you've excavated and poured a walkway, you can confidently take on larger concrete projects, such as patios and driveways.

This project shows you how to lay out the site (including any turns you want to incorporate), excavate and build forms, lay down a gravel subbase, and pour and work the concrete. For more information on these steps, and the most effective techniques, consult the section on concrete in Masonry Techniques (pages 16 to 61).

Everything You Need:

Tools: Line level, hammer, shovel, sod cutter, wheelbarrow, tamper, drill, level, screed board, straightedge, mason's string, mason's float, mason's trowel, edger, groover, stiff-bristle broom.

Materials: Garden stakes, rebar, bolsters, 2 × 4 lumber, 2½" and 3" screws, concrete mix, concrete sealer, isolation board, compactible gravel, construction adhesive, nails.

How to Pour a Concrete Walkway

1 Select a rough layout, including any turns. Stake out the location and connect the stakes with mason's strings. Set the slope, if needed (page 25). Remove sod between and 6" beyond the lines, then excavate the site with a spade to a depth 4" greater than the thickness of the concrete walkway, following the slope lines to maintain consistent depth.

2 Pour a 5" layer of compactible gravel as a subbase for the walkway. Tamp the subbase until it compacts to an even 4" thick layer (page 25).

3 Build and install 2 × 4 forms set on edge (page 26). Miter-cut the ends at angled joints. Position them so the inside edges are lined up with the strings. Attach the forms with 3" deck screws, then drive 2 × 4 stakes next to the forms at 3-ft. intervals. Attach the stakes to the forms with 2½" deck screws. Use a level to make sure forms are level or set to achieve the desired slope. Drive stakes at each side of angled joints.

4 Glue an isolation board (page 23) to the steps, house foundation, or other permanent structures that adjoin the walkway, using construction adhesive.

OPTION: Reinforce the walkway with #3 steel rebar. For a 3-ft.-wide walkway, lay two sections of rebar spaced evenly inside the project area. Use bolsters to support the rebar (make sure rebar is at least 2" below the tops of the forms). Bend rebar to follow any angles or curves, and overlap pieces at angled joints by 12". Mark locations for control joints (to be cut with a groover later) by tacking nails to the outside faces of the forms, spaced roughly at 3-ft. intervals.

(continued next page)

5 Mix, then pour concrete into the project area (pages 32 to 33). Use a masonry hoe to spread it evenly within the forms. After pouring all of the concrete, run a spade along the inside edges of the form, then rap the outside edges of the forms with a hammer to help settle the concrete.

6 Build a curved screed board (page 65) and use it to form a crown when you smooth out the concrete. NOTE: A helper makes this easier.

7 Smooth the surface with a float (page 35). Cut control joints at marked locations (page 34), using a trowel and a straightedge. Let the concrete dry until any bleed water disappears.

8 Shape the edges of the concrete by running an edger along the forms. Smooth out any marks created by the edger, using a float. Lift the leading edges of the edger and float slightly as you work.

9 Once any bleed water has disappeared, draw a groover along the control joints, using a straight 2 × 4 as a guide. Use a float to smooth out any tool marks.

10 Create a textured, non-skid surface by drawing a clean, stiff-bristled broom across the surface (page 52). Avoid overlapping broom marks. Cover the walkway with plastic and let the concrete cure for one week.

11 Remove the forms, then backfill the space at the sides of the walkway with dirt or sod. Seal the concrete, if desired, according to the manufacturer's directions.

Laying a Flagstone Walkway

With flagstone, sand, and wood edging, you can create a walkway that is durable enough to withstand heavy traffic while maintaining a natural ambience. You can pave a flagstone walkway from start to finish in less than a day. The only maintenance for a sand-set flagstone walkway involves sweeping new sand into the joints every year or two to compensate for erosion and settling.

Everything You Need:

Tools: Garden rake, drill, maul, pitching chisel, circular saw with masonry blade, rubber mallet.

Materials: 2 × 6 lumber (pressure-treated lumber, redwood or cedar), pressure-treated wood stakes, 2½" galvanized screws, compactible gravel, landscape fabric, mason's sand, flagstone.

Test-fit flagstone to find an attractive arrangement that minimizes the amount of splitting required. Leave ⅜" to 2" gaps between stones. Use chalk to mark stones for cutting, then remove the stones and split them, as needed, on a flat surface (pages 46 to 49).

How to Build a Flagstone Walkway

1 Outline the walkway site and excavate to a depth of 6". Allow enough room for the edging and stakes (step 2). For straight walkways, use stakes and strings to maintain a uniform outline. Add a 2" layer of compactible gravel subbase, using a rake to smooth the surface.

2 Install 2 × 6 edging made from pressure-treated lumber around the sides of the site. Drive 12" stakes on the outside of the edging, spaced 12" apart. The tops of the stakes should be below ground level. Attach the edging to the stakes, using galvanized screws.

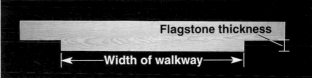

Flagstone thickness

Width of walkway

3 Lay sheets of landscape fabric over the walkway site to prevent weeds and grass from growing up between the stones. (Omit the landscape fabric if you want to plant grass seed or ground cover to fill the cracks). Spread a 2" layer of sand over the landscape fabric to serve as a base for the flagstones.

4 Make a screed board for smoothing the sand by notching the ends of a short 2 × 6 to fit inside the edging (bottom photo). The depth of the notches should equal the thickness of the stones, usually about 2". Screed the base by pulling the 2 × 6 from one end of the walkway to the other. Add more sand as needed until the base is smooth.

5 Beginning at one corner of the walkway, lay the flagstones onto the sand base so the gap between stones is at least ⅜", but no more than 2". If needed, add or remove sand beneath stones to level them. Set the stones by tapping them with a rubber mallet or a length of 2 × 6.

6 Fill the gaps between stones with sand. (Use soil if you are planting grass or ground cover in the cracks.) Pack the sand with your fingers or a piece of scrap wood, then spray the walkway lightly with water to help the sand settle. Add new sand as necessary until gaps are filled.

Riser

Tread

Simple garden steps can be built by making a series of concrete platforms framed with 5 × 6 timbers. Garden steps have shorter vertical risers and deeper horizontal treads than the outdoor stairs that lead to the threshold of your home. Risers for garden stairs should be no more than 6", and treads should be at least 11" deep.

Building Garden Steps

Garden steps make sloping yards safer and more accessible. They also introduce new combinations of materials into your landscape.

You can build garden steps with a variety of materials, including flagstones, brick, timbers, concrete block, or poured concrete. Whatever materials you use, make sure the steps are level and firmly anchored so they're easy to climb and offer good traction. If you're finishing the steps with concrete, review "Finishing & Curing Concrete" (pages 36 to 37) before you begin pouring.

Everything You Need:

Tools: Maul, chain saw or reciprocating saw with 12" wood-cutting blade, tape measure, level, mason's string, hammer, shovel, drill with 1" spade bit and bit extension, garden rake, mason's trowel, wheelbarrow, mason's hoe, carpenter's square, float, edging tool, stiff-bristle brush.

Materials: 1 × 4 lumber, 1" screws, 5 × 6 landscape timbers, ¾" interior dia. black pipe, 12" galvanized spikes, concrete mix, compactible gravel, seed gravel (½" max. dia.), 2 × 4 board, plastic sheeting, burlap.

Tips for Mixing Concrete

For large amounts (more than ½ cu. yd.), you can mix your own concrete in a wheelbarrow or rented mixer. Use a ratio of 1 part portland cement (A), 2 parts sand (B), and 3 parts gravel (C). See page 9 to estimate the amount of concrete needed.

For small amounts (less than ½ cu. yd.), buy premixed bags of dry concrete). A 60-lb. bag of concrete mix yields about ½ cu. ft. of concrete. A masonry hoe with holes in the blade is useful for mixing concrete.

Tips for Building Garden Steps

⅛" downward pitch per foot

Build a slight downward pitch into outdoor steps so water will drain off without puddling. Do not exceed a pitch of ⅛" per foot.

Order custom-cut timbers to reduce installation time if the dimensions of each step are identical. Some building supply centers charge a small fee for custom-cutting timbers.

How to Plan Garden Steps

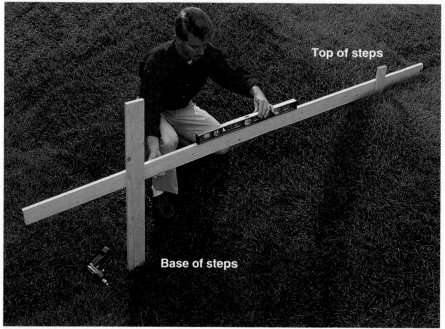

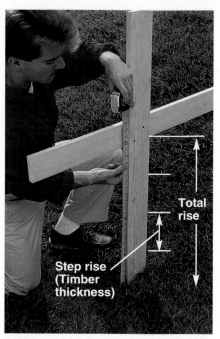

1 Drive a tall stake into the ground at the base of the stairway site. Adjust the stake so it is exactly plumb. Drive a shorter stake at the top of the site. Position a long, straight 1 × 4 against the stakes, with one end touching the ground next to the top stake. Adjust the 1 × 4 so it is level, then attach it to the stakes with screws. (For long spans, use a mason's string instead of a 1 × 4.)

2 Measure from the ground to the bottom of the 1 × 4 to find the total vertical rise of the stairway. Divide the rise by the actual thickness of the timbers (about 6" if using 5 × 6 timbers) to find the number of steps required. Round off any fractions.

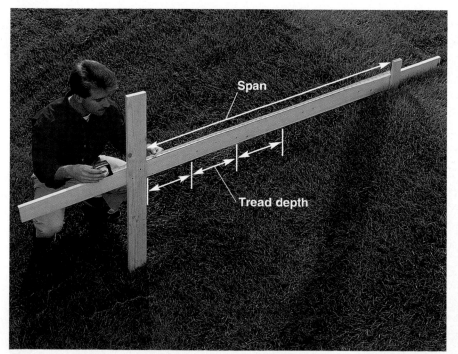

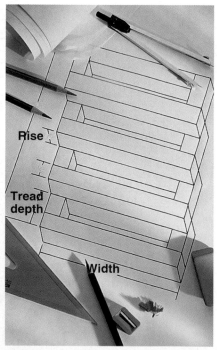

3 Measure along the 1 × 4 between the stakes to find the total horizontal span. Divide the span by the number of steps to find the depth of each step tread. If depth is less than 11", revise the step layout to extend the depth of the step treads.

4 Make a sketch of the step site, showing rise, tread depth, and width of each step. Remember that actual timber dimensions may vary from the nominal measurements.

How to Build Garden Steps Using Timbers & Concrete

1 Mark the sides of the step site with stakes and string. The stakes should be positioned at the front edge of the bottom step and the back edge of the top step.

Tread depth

2 Add the width of a timber (about 5") to the tread depth, then measure back this distance from the stakes and drive additional stakes to mark the back edge of the first step. Connect these stakes with string to mark the digging area for the first step.

3 Excavate for the first step, creating a flat bed with a very slight forward slope, no more than ⅛" from back to front. The front of the excavation should be no more than 2" deep. Tamp the soil firmly.

4 For each step, use a chain saw or reciprocating saw to cut a front timber equal to the step width, a back timber 10" shorter, and two side timbers equal to the tread depth.

(continued next page)

5 Arrange the timbers to form the step frame, drill pilot holes, and end-nail the timbers together by driving 12" spikes into the pilot holes.

6 Set the timber frame in position. Use a carpenter's square to make sure the frame is square, and adjust as necessary. Drill two 1" pilot holes in the front timber and the back timber, 1 ft. from the ends, using a spade bit and bit extension.

7 Anchor the steps to the ground by driving a 2½-ft. length of ¾" pipe through each pilot hole until the pipe is flush with the timber. When pipes are driven, make sure the frame is level from side to side and has the proper forward pitch. Excavate for the next step, making sure the bottom of the excavation is even with top edge of the installed timbers.

Drive pipes here

8 Build another step frame and position it in the excavation so the front timber is directly over the rear timber on the first frame. Drill pilot holes, then nail the steps together with three 12" spikes. Drill pilot holes for two pipes, then drive two pipes through only the back timber to anchor the second frame.

9 Continue digging and installing the remaining frames until the steps reach full height. The back of the last step should be at ground level.

10 Staple plastic over the timbers to protect them from wet concrete. Cut away the plastic so it does not overhang into the frame opening.

11 Pour a 2" layer of compactible gravel into each frame as a subbase, and use a 2 × 4 to tamp it down.

12 Mix concrete in a wheelbarrow, adding just enough water so the concrete holds its shape when sliced with a trowel. NOTE: To save time and labor, you can have ready-mix concrete delivered to the site. Many ready-mix companies will deliver concrete in amounts as small as ⅓ cu. yd. (enough for three steps of the type shown here).

13 Shovel concrete into the bottom frame, flush with the top of the timbers. Work the concrete lightly with a garden rake to help remove air bubbles, but do not overwork the concrete.

(continued next page)

14 Smooth (screed) the concrete by dragging a 2 × 4 across the top of the frame. If necessary, add concrete to low areas and screed again until the surface is smooth and free of low spots.

15 While the concrete is still wet, seed it by scattering mixed gravel onto the surface. Sand-and-gravel suppliers and garden centers sell colorful gravel designed for seeding. For best results, select a mixture with stones no larger than ½" in diameter.

16 Press the seeded gravel into the surface of the concrete, using a float, until the tops of the stones are flush with the surface of the concrete. Remove any concrete that spills over the edges of the frame, using a trowel.

17 Pour concrete into remaining steps, screeding and seeding each step before moving on to the next. Remember to let any bleed water evaporate before seeding. For a neat appearance, use an edging tool (inset) to shape seams between the timbers and the concrete as you complete each step.

18 Let any bleed water disappear. This may take from 30 minutes to several hours, depending on weather conditions. Use a float to smooth out any high or low spots in each step. NOTE: Overfloating (page 35) can force gravel too far into the concrete. Let the concrete dry for about an hour.

19 Apply a fine mist of water to the surface, then scrub it with a stiff brush to expose the seeded gravel.

VARIATION: To save time and money, skip the seeding procedure. Work the concrete, then drag a push broom across it. To achieve a finer texture and a more weather-resistant surface, wait until the concrete is firm to the touch before using the broom technique.

20 Remove the plastic and cover the concrete with burlap. Allow concrete to cure for a week, spraying it occasionally with water to ensure even curing. NOTE: Concrete can be cleaned from timbers using a 5 percent solution of muriatic acid and water, but the solution may change the color of the timbers.

Pre-cast concrete step forms make it easy to build a durable outdoor staircase. By overlapping the forms in varying arrangements, you can shape a staircase with curves, angles, and even spirals. Lay two forms side-by-side to create larger steps.

Building Steps with Pre-cast Forms

Pre-cast concrete step forms are ideal for building attractive steps without having to build wood forms and pour the concrete yourself. In a few hours, you can excavate, lay pre-cast forms, and pour in concrete. Or, pour a sand bed inside the forms and fill them with brick pavers (above).

Many manufacturers sell pavers that are sized to fit inside the forms they make. Decide how many forms you'll need for the steps you plan to build and the paver pattern you wish to use, then consult the manufacturer's specifications to determine the number of pavers required.

To plan the layout for this project, follow steps 1 to 4 on page 74. You can adjust the amount of overlap for each step to fit the dimensions of your site or to create a desired appearance.

Everything You Need:

Tools: Mason's string, drill, level, shovel, rake, hand tamper, tape measure, rubber mallet, broom.

Materials: Straight 2 × 4 board, stakes, screws, concrete step forms, pavers, compactible gravel, sand.

How to Build Steps with Pre-cast Forms

1 Mark the outline of your steps with stakes and string, then excavate for the first step. Dig a hole 6" deeper than the height of the step and 4" wider and longer than the step on all sides.

2 Fill the hole with compactible gravel. Rake the gravel to create a slight downward slope (⅛" per foot) from back to front, for drainage. Tamp it well with a hand tamper, then set the first form in place. Use a level to make sure the form is level from side to side and has the proper slope from back to front.

3 Add a layer of gravel inside the form and tamp it well. The distance between the gravel and the top of the form should equal the thickness of a paver plus 1". Next, add a 1"-thick layer of sand over the gravel. Use a 2 × 4 set across the form to measure as you go.

4 Lay the pavers in the form in the desired pattern, keeping them level with the top of the form. Adjust as needed, using a rubber mallet or by adding sand underneath. Use a broom to spread sand over the pavers to fill the joints.

5 Excavate for the next step, accounting for the overlap and a 4" space behind and at the sides for gravel. Fill and tamp the gravel so the front is level with the top of the first step. Repeat steps 2 to 4. When all steps are installed, backfill with dirt along the sides.

Apron

Control joint (for driveways wider than 10 ft.)

Isolation joint or Control joint

Find the slope of your current driveway by dividing the length in feet (the horizontal distance from the apron to the curb) by the vertical drop in inches. This tells you how many inches per foot the new driveway should slope. It's easiest to use a water level (page 87) to measure the vertical drop. Joints cut in the driveway's surface or created with strips of felt placed between sections of the driveway reduce damage from cracking and buckling. A crowned surface encourages water to run off to the sides.

Pouring a Concrete Driveway

Pouring a driveway is a lot like pouring a patio or walk, but on a larger scale. It's particularly useful to divide the driveway into sections that you can pour one at a time. A wood divider (page 84) is removed after each section is firm and repositioned to pour the next section. For driveways wider than 10 ft., a control joint is added down the center to keep cracks from spreading. Driveways up to 10 ft. wide are simplest because you can pour fiber-reinforced concrete directly over the subbase without additional reinforcement. (Check with your building inspector regarding local requirements.) For a larger slab, add metal reinforcement, using the approach used for a walkway (page 66).

Pay attention to drainage conditions when planning your driveway. Soil that drains poorly can damage a slab. If drainage is poor, line your site with polyethylene sheeting before pouring. It is

Everything You Need:

Tools: Level, water level, mason's string, screed board, mallet, wheelbarrow, circular saw, drill, broom, coarse brush, hand float, concrete edger and groover, darby, shovel, wheelbarrow, hoe, spade, hammer, trowel, edger, bucket, measuring tape, hand tamper or power tamper.

Materials: Stakes, 2 x 4 and 1 x 2 lumber, crushed stone, fiber-reinforced concrete mix, 4"-wide bituminous felt, 2" deck screws, vegetable oil or commercial release agent, 6 mil plastic sheeting.

critical to establish a gradual slope, using the approach shown in the photo above and a crowned surface, so water runs off the driveway. NOTE: It's important to handle bleed water carefully as you pour a driveway. Review the section on bleed water (page 35) before beginning your project.

How to Lay Out a Driveway Slab

Laying Out the Site

A proper layout is key to determining how well your driveway functions. Start by calculating the amount of drop per foot on the site. You need this number so you can maintain a gradual slope as you excavate. Plan to excavate an area 10" wider than the slab. This allows room for stakes and forms that will hold the concrete in place. How deep you need to dig depends on the thickness of the slab and the subbase, typically 4" each. (Check with your building inspector. Building Codes in some areas call for a 6" slab—in that case, you'll need 2 × 6s instead of 2 × 4s for forms.) Use beveled 12" 1 × 2 stakes and mason's strings to mark the edges of the site. Set the stakes at a consistent height so you can use them to check the depth of the excavated site.

8" (minimum depth)

1 Excavate the site (pages 24 to 25), using stakes and mason's strings to establish the proper slope. You may have to remove the stakes temporarily to smooth the bottom of the site with a 2 × 4 and pack the soil with a tamper.

2 Pour a 4" layer of crushed stone as a subbase. Screed with a long 2 × 4, then tamp the stone. You can make small adjustments to the slope of the site, as required, by adjusting the thickness of the subbase.

3½"

3 Drive stakes at the corners of the site, 3½" in from each side. Connect the stakes on each side with mason's strings. Use a water level (inset, right) to check that the strings are set to the correct slope. Adjust the stakes as necessary.

4 Position 2 × 4 forms inside the strings with the tops level with the strings. Plant stakes every 2 ft. outside the forms, with the tops slightly lower than the tops of the forms. Drive deck screws through the stakes and into the forms. Where forms meet (above), secure them to a single 1 × 4 stake.

(continued next page)

How to Lay Out a Driveway Slab (continued)

Option: Use 1 × 4s to create forms for turns in the driveway. Saw parallel ½"-deep kerfs in one side of each board, and bend the boards to form the proper curves. Attach the curved forms inside the stakes. Backfill beneath all of the forms.

⅝"
**spacer
between
boards**

5 Construct a divider equal in length to the width of the slab. Set a 1 × 2 on the edge of a 2 × 4; place a ⅝" × 1½" wood spacer midway between them, flush with the edges. Attach the two pieces with 2" deck screws so the screw heads sink below the surface. The curved top of the divider will form the crown of the driveway as you screed.

6 Position the divider roughly 6 ft. from the top of the driveway. Drive screws through the forms and into the divider to hold it in place temporarily. Place a felt isolation strip against the divider. Prop the strip in place temporarily with bricks. NOTE: If your site drains poorly, add a layer of polyethylene over the bottom of the site as a vapor barrier.

7 Coat the dividers and forms with vegetable oil or commercial release agent so concrete won't bond to their surfaces as it cures. Mix fiber-reinforced concrete for one section of the slab at a time, using a power mixer, or order concrete from a ready-mix supplier. If you use ready-mix, have helpers on hand so you can pour the concrete as soon as it arrives.

How to Pour a Driveway Slab

1 Pour pods of concrete (pages 32 to 33) into the first section, digging into the concrete with a shovel to eliminate air pockets. Remove the brick props inside the site once there is sufficient concrete in place to prop up the felt strip.

2 Screed the concrete from side to side, using a 2 × 4 resting on the driveway apron and the crowned divider. Raise the leading edge of the board slightly as you move it across the concrete. Add concrete to any low spots. Rescreed if necessary.

3 Float the surface with a darby, then let the surface cure for 2-4 hours, or until it is solid enough to support your weight. NOTE: For a slab wider than 10 ft., cut a control joint down the slab's center line.

4 Use an edger along the inside of the forms to create smooth edges (page 35). Remove the divider and screw it in place alongside a felt strip to pour the next section. Screw the divider in place and prop it with bricks.

5 Finish the surface as desired as each section hardens (page 36). Cover the sections with polyethylene sheeting, misting daily for two weeks. Remove the forms and seal the concrete.

Cut stone is a top-quality material for building walls, pillars and arches. For retaining walls (shown above) cut stone or interlocking block is laid without mortar (except for the top course) so water doesn't become trapped behind the wall. Free-standing structures are often built with mortar. Either method can be used to build walls that will last for generations. Both are described in this section.

Walls, Pillars & Arches

Vertical masonry structures can be as simple or as grand as you chose. Because of the strength and durability of masonry, you are limited only by your imagination, time, and energy. The projects presented here include some of the easiest and most popular—from constructing a concrete block wall with an attractive finish, to building sturdy brick pillars. Also included are more challenging projects that add a touch of elegance. They include a brick arch and a stone wall with a *moon window*. Even these projects are surprisingly easy if you approach them patiently. Of course, you don't have to use the identical materials. You can construct your arch with stone or build a moon window with brick. Before starting, read the sections under Masonry Techniques devoted to the materials you plan to use.

Finished with stucco and topped with lattice panels, this concrete block wall forms an attractive divider between a patio and yard.

How to Lay Out a Wall, Pillar, or Arch

1 To get a sense of the size and impact of a wall or other project before you begin construction, plot the borders of the project, using tall stakes or poles, then tie mason's strings marking the projected top of the structure.

2 Hang landscape fabric or sheets of plastic between the stakes and over the top of the string. View the structure from all sides for an indication of how much it will obstruct views and access, and how it will blend with other elements of the landscape.

Working with a Water Level

Water levels take advantage of the fact that water in an open tube will level itself, no matter how many bends and turns the tube has. This makes a water level ideal for working with long structures, around corners, or on sites where a conventional level won't work. Typical commercially available water levels consist of clear plastic tubes that screw onto the ends of a garden hose (right, top). Mark off 1" increments on each tube. Attach the tubes to the ends of a garden hose, then fill the hose until water is visible in both tubes. Working with a helper, hold the tubes at the ends of the site. Adjust the tubes until the water is at the same mark in each tube (right, bottom). Drive stakes or mark off the level points on your structure. OPTION: Pricier water levels contain an electronic gauge that's useful when you need precise readings.

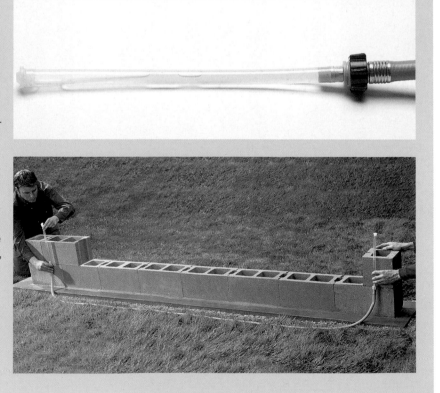

How to Plot a Right Angle

1 The 3-4-5 triangle method is the most effective method of plotting right angles for walls, pillars, and other construction. Begin by staking the outside corner of your walls and stringing a mason's string to mark the outside of one wall.

2 Mark a point 3 ft. out along that wall by planting another stake.

3 Position the end of one tape measure at the outside corner and open it past the 4 ft. mark. Have an assistant position the end of another tape measure at the 3 ft. stake and open it past the 5 ft. mark. Lock the tape measures and adjust them so they intersect at the 4 ft. and 5 ft. marks.

4 Plant a stake at the meeting point, then run mason's strings from this stake to the outside corner. The 3 ft. and 4 ft. mason's strings form a right angle. Extend or shorten the mason's strings, as required, and stake out the exact dimensions of your structure.

How to Plot a Curve

1 Start by plotting a right angle, using the 3-4-5 triangle method (opposite page). Mark the end points for the curve by measuring and planting stakes equidistant from the outside corner.

2 Tie a mason's string to those stakes. Extend each string back to the outside corner, then hold them tight at the point where they meet. Pull this point toward the inside of the angle until the strings are taut. The strings will complete a square.

3 Plant a stake at their meeting point, then tie a piece of mason's string to that stake, just long enough to reach the stakes marking the endpoints of the curve.

4 Pull the string taut, then swing it in an arc between the end points, using spray paint to mark the curve on the ground.

Begin a freestanding block wall project with a properly sized footing (pages 38 to 41).

Building Freestanding Block Walls without Mortar

The project below shows how to lay a block wall without using mortar between blocks. Mortarless walls are built using a running bond pattern, and are simple to construct. They derive their strength from a coating of surface bonding cement on all exposed surfaces. The cement creates a bond between blocks that is strong enough to support even very long walls. The coating is similar in appearance and workability to stucco, so you can achieve an attractive stucco wall look.

Concrete block walls can also be built with mortar. This is the only option if you're using decorative block or if you want to leave the blocks exposed.

Everything You Need:

Tools: Aviation snips, mason's trowel, brickset chisel, maul, mason's string, level, chalk line, line blocks.

Materials: Concrete block, metal ties, wire mesh, type N mortar, surface bonding cement.

How to Lay a Mortarless Block Wall

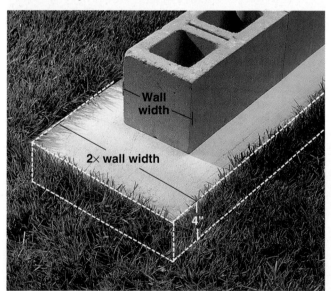

1 Start with a dry layout of the first course on a concrete footing. Where less than half a block is needed, trim two blocks instead. For example, where 3⅓ block lengths are required, use four blocks, and cut two of them to ⅔ their length. You'll end up with a stronger, more durable wall.

2 Mark the corners of the end blocks on the footing with a pencil. Then, remove the blocks and snap chalk lines to indicate where to lay the mortar bed and the initial course of block.

3 Mist the footing with water, then lay a ⅜"-thick bed of mortar on the footing. Take care to cover only the area inside the reference lines.

4 Lay the first course, starting at one end and placing blocks in the mortar bed with no spacing in between blocks. Use solid-faced block on the ends of the wall, and check the course for level.

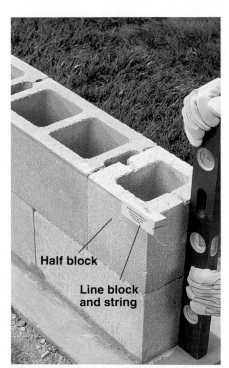

Half block

Line block and string

5 Lay subsequent courses one at a time, using a level to check for plumb and line blocks to check for level. Begin courses with solid-face blocks at each end. Use half blocks, to establish a running bond pattern.

6 If a block requires leveling, cut a piece of corrugated metal tie and slip it underneath. If a block is off by more than ⅛", remove the block, trowel a dab of mortar underneath, and reposition the block.

7 Lay wire mesh over the next to last course. Install the top course, then fill block hollows with mortar and trowel the surface smooth.

(continued next page)

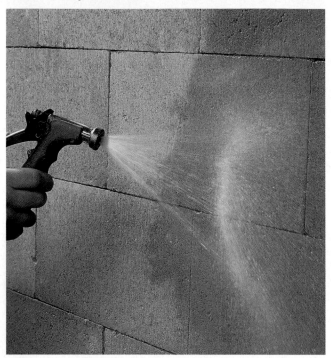

8 Starting near the top of the wall, mist a 2 × 5 ft. section on one side of the wall with water to prevent the blocks from absorbing moisture from the cement once the coating is applied.

9 Mix the cement in small batches, according to the manufacturer's instructions, and apply a 1/16"- to 1/8"-thick layer to the damp blocks, using a square-end trowel. Spread the cement evenly by angling the trowel slightly and making broad upward strokes.

10 Use a wet trowel to smooth the surface, and to create the texture of your choice. Rinse the trowel frequently to keep it clean and wet.

11 To prevent random cracking, use a groover (page 34) to cut control joints from top to bottom, every 4 ft. for a 2-ft.-high wall, every 8 ft. for a 4-ft.-high wall. Seal the hardened joints with silicone caulk.

This low patio wall, made with 8 × 8" glass block mortared between concrete block support columns, provides an attractive wind break for an outdoor sitting area while allowing light to pass through.

Building a Glass Block Wall

You may not think of glass as a masonry product, but building a glass block wall is much like laying a mortared brick wall, with two important differences. First, a glass block wall must be supported by another structure and cannot function as a load-bearing wall. Second, glass block cannot be cut, so lay out your project carefully.

You can find glass block, along with a few products that help with the installation, at a specialty distributor or home center. For straight wall sections, use plastic spacers between blocks. The spacers ensure consistent mortar joints and support the weight of the block to prevent mortar from squeezing out before it sets. You'll also find colored glass block (type N) mortar and tints for coloring standard type N mortar. Mix the mortar a little drier than you would for brick; glass won't wick water out of the mortar like brick does.

Because there are many applications for glass block and installation techniques may vary from project to project, ask a glass block retailer or manufacturer for advice about the best products and methods for your project.

Glass block sizes and styles include: bullnose end and corner blocks for finishing exposed edges, and radial blocks for right angles or curves. Glass block textures and patterns offer varying degrees of privacy.

Everything You Need:

Tools: Trowel, level, wire cutters, jointing tool, sponge, pail, nylon-bristle brush, cloth.

Materials: Glass block (8 × 8"), glass block spacers, panel reinforcing wire, anchors, concrete block (6 × 8 × 8"), glass block mortar, type N mortar, 6"-wide capstone, brick sealer.

Building Entryway Pillars

Freestanding pillars are easy to design because you don't have to be concerned about the seasonal shifting of attached walls or other structures. We designed a pair of 12 × 16" pillars using only whole bricks, so you don't need to worry about splitting. These pillars are refined in appearance, but sturdy enough to last for decades.

Once the last course of bricks is in place, you can add a brick or stone cap for a finished look. Or, build two pillars connected by an arch (pages 100 to 103). If you're planning an arch, consider attaching hardware for an iron gate (page 19). It's far easier to place the hardware in fresh mortar, so make a note of the brick courses where the hardware will go. The settings will look cleaner this way, and the hardware will stay secure for a long time.

This 4-ft. pillar was built with 18 courses of brick. A brick cap adds a touch of elegance and protects against rain, ice and snow. You can also build pillars with stone caps, or, as shown on the following pages, use cast concrete caps, which are available in many sizes.

Pour footings (pages 38 to 41) that are 4" longer and wider than the pillars on each side. This project calls for 16 × 20" footings.

Everything You Need:

Tools: Level, bricklayer's trowel, jointing tool, aviation snips, wheelbarrow, shovel, hoe, tape measure, pointing chisel.

Materials: Standard modular bricks (4 × 2⅔ × 8"), dowel, type N mortar mix, ¼" wire mesh, capstone or concrete cap, 2 × 2 lumber, ⅜"-thick wood scraps.

Tips for Building Brick Pillars

Use a story pole to maintain consistent mortar joint thickness. Line up a scrap 2 × 2 on a flat tabletop alongside a column of bricks, spaced ⅜" apart. Mark the identical spacing on the 2 × 4. Hold up pole after every few courses to check the mortar joints for consistent thickness.

Cut a straight 2 × 2 to fit tight in the space between the two pillars. As you lay each course for the second pillar, use the 2 × 2 to check the span.

How to Build Brick Pillars

1 Once the footing has cured, dry-lay the first course of five bricks, centered on the footing. Mark reference lines around the bricks.

2 Lay a bed of mortar inside the reference lines and lay the first course.

(continued next page)

If you're building an arch over existing pillars, measure the distance between the pillars at several points. The span must be the same at each point in order for the pillars to serve as strong supports for your arch.

Adding an Arch to Entryway Pillars

Building an arch over a pair of pillars is a challenging task made easier with a simple, semi-circular plywood form. With the form in place, you can create a symmetrical arch by laying bricks along the form's curved edge. Select bricks equal in length to those used in the pillars.

When building new pillars (pages 96 to 99), use the colors and textures of your home exterior and landscape to guide your choice of brick. Brickyards sell mortar tint to complement the color of your bricks. Once you settle on the amount of tint to add to the mortar, record the recipe, so you can maintain a consistent color in every batch.

Everything You Need:

Tools: Joint chisel, mason's hammer, pry bar, jig saw, circular saw, drill, compass, level, mason's string, trowel, jointing tool, tuck-pointer.

Materials: ¾" plywood, ¼" plywood, wallboard screws (1" and 2"), bricks, type N mortar mix, 2 × 4 and 2 × 8 lumber, shims.

How to Build a Form for an Arch

1 Determine the distance between the inside edges of the tops of your pillars. Divide the distance in half, then subtract ¼". Use this as the radius in step 2.

2 Mark a point at the center of a sheet of ¾" plywood. Use a pencil and a piece of string to scribe the circle on the plywood, using the radius calculated in step 1. Cut out the circle with a jigsaw. Then mark a line through the center point of the circle and cut the circle in half with a jig saw or a circular saw.

3 Construct the form by bracing the two semicircles, using 2" wallboard screws and 2 × 4s. To calculate the length of the 2 × 4 braces, subtract the combined thickness of the plywood sheets — 1½"—from the width of the pillars, and cut the braces to length. Cover the top of the form with ¼" plywood, attached with 1" wallboard screws.

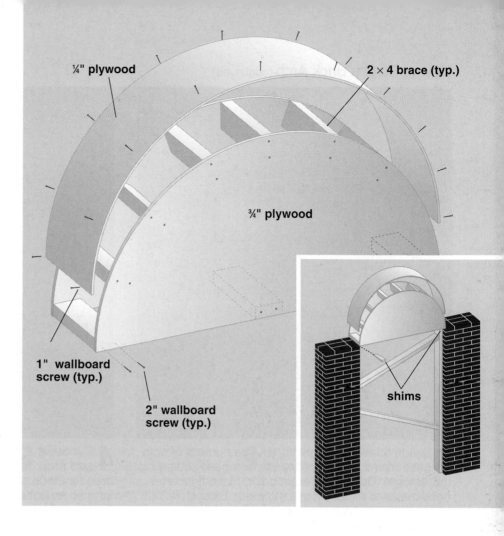

¼" plywood

2 × 4 brace (typ.)

¾" plywood

1" wallboard screw (typ.)

2" wallboard screw (typ.)

shims

How to Build a Brick Arch

Tip: If your pillars are capped, remove the caps before building an arch. Chip out the old mortar from underneath, using a hammer and joint chisel. With a helper nearby to support the cap, use a pry bar and shims to remove each cap from the pillar.

1 To determine brick spacing, start by centering a brick at the peak and placing a compass point at one edge. With the compass set to the width of one brick plus ¼", mark the form with the pencil.

2 Place the compass point on this new mark and make another mark along the curve. Continue making marks along the curve until less than a brick's width remains.

(continued next page)

A moon window is just about the most dramatic garden element you can build. We constructed the wall shown here using cut ashlar mortared around a semicircular form, but using brick is also an option. Once the bottom half of the window has set up, the form is flipped and the top stones are placed. The construction technique for the form is the same one used in building an arch (pages 100 to 103).

Building a Stone Moon Window

You can build circular openings into brick or stone walls, using a single semicircular wood form. Moon windows can be built to any dimension, although lifting and placing stones is more difficult as the project grows larger, while tapering stones to fit is a greater challenge as the circle gets smaller. To minimize the need for cutting and lifting stone, we built this window 2 ft. in diameter atop an existing stone wall. Before doing this, you'll need to check with your local building inspector regarding restrictions on wall height, footings (pages 38 to 41), and other design considerations. You may need to modify the dimensions to conform with the local Building Code.

Make sure to have at least one helper on hand. Building with stone is always physically demanding, and steps such as installing the brace and form (opposite page) require a helper.

Everything You Need:

Tools: Jig saw, circular saw, drill, tape measure, level, mortar box, mason's hoe, trowels, jointing tool or tuck-pointer, mortar bag, stone chisel, maul.

Materials: ¾" plywood, ¼" plywood, wallboard screws (1" and 2"), tapered shims, 2 × 4 and 2 × 8 lumber, 4 × 4 posts, type M mortar (stiff mix), ashlar stone.

How to Build a Stone Moon Window

1 Build a plywood form, following the instructions on page 99. Select stones for the top of the circle with sides that are squared off or slightly tapered. Dry-lay the stones around the outside of the form, spacing the stones with shims that are roughly ¼" thick at their narrow end.

2 Number each stone and a corresponding point on the form, using chalk, then set the stones aside. Turn the form around, and label a second set of stones for the bottom of the circle. Tip: to avoid confusion, use letters to label the bottom set of stones instead of numbers.

3 Prepare a stiff mix of type M mortar (pages 16 to 19 and lay a ½"-thick mortar bed on top of the wall for the base of the circle. Center the stone that will be at the base of the circle in the mortar.

4 Set the form on top of the stone, and brace the form by constructing a sturdy 2 × 4 scaffold and secure it by constructing a bracing structure made from 4 × 4 posts and 2 × 4 lumber. We used pairs of 2 × 4s nailed together for lengthwise supports. Check the form for level in both directions, and adjust the braces as required. Screw the braces to the form, so the edges are at least ¼" in from the edges of the form.

(continued next page)

5 Extend the mortar bed along the wall and add stones, buttering one end of each stone, and tapping them into place with a trowel. Keep the joint width consistent with the existing wall, but set the depth of new joints at about 1", to allow for tuck-pointing.

6 Attach mason's string at the center of the front and back of the form and use the strings to check the alignment of each stone.

7 Stagger the joints as you build upward and outward. Alternate large and small stones for maximum strength and a natural look. Stop occasionally to smooth joints that have hardened enough to resist minimal finger pressure.

8 If large bumps or curves interfere as you lay stones around the circle, dress those stones (pages 46 to 49), as necessary, so the sides are roughly squared off.

9 Once you've laid stones about ½" beyond the top edge of the form, disassemble the bracing.

10 Invert the form on top of the wall in preparation for laying the top half of the circle. The bottom edge of the form should be set roughly ½" higher than the top of the lower half of the circle. Check the braces for level (both lengthwise and widthwise), and adjust them as necessary and reattach them to the posts.

11 Lay stones around the circle, working from the bottom up, so the top, or keystone, is laid last. If mortar oozes from the joints, insert temporary shims. Remove the shims after 2 hours, and pack the voids with mortar.

12 Once the keystone is in place, smooth the remaining joints. Let the wall set up overnight, then mist it several times a day for a week. Remove the form.

13 Remove any excess mortar from the joints inside the circle. Mist lightly, then tuck-point all joints with stiff mortar so they are of equal depth.

14 Once the joints reach a putty-like consistency, tool them with a jointing tool. Let the mortar harden overnight. Mist the wall for five more days.

Update the exterior of your house with brick, stone or stucco veneer. Whether installed to cover an unattractive foundation or to accent an otherwise ordinary exterior, veneers add color and texture to your house. They also add weight to a wall, so ask an inspector about Building Code rules before you start.

Finishing House & Garden Walls

Masonry materials are ideal for protecting and enhancing the look of exterior walls, both new and old. If you build an addition, you can use stucco to match or complement the materials on existing walls. Stucco is also easy to repair or restore. Thin veneers of natural or manufactured stone are growing rapidly in popularity because they are easy to work with and add a touch of grandeur to any structure. These materials all work well on garden walls, too. With brick, stone, or stucco, you can turn an ordinary concrete block wall into an attractive element of your garden. With concrete block and super-strong surface bonding cement (page 92), you can build a wall with a stucco-style surface, using no mortar at all.

Tips for Planning:

• Use brick or stone veneer as a decorative accent on the front face or entry area of your house. Installing veneer around an entire house is a demanding project best left to a professional.

• Ask your local building inspector about allowable height, reinforcement, use of wall ties, space between veneer and wall sheathing, drainage, and specifications for metal support shelves. A building permit may be required.

• Cut bricks before you start. With stone, do a dry run on a flat surface before you start.

• Examine the area around your foundation. Builders often install a concrete ledge just below grade as a base for veneer. If your house has no base, attach a metal support shelf to the foundation.

Options for Finishing Exterior Walls

Renew an old foundation by applying brick or stone veneer from ground level up to the sill plate. The foundation must be free from structural damage.

Veneer stone may consist of thin cuts of quarried stone or tinted concrete blocks that look like natural stone but are lighter and easier to install.

Full-wall veneer is applied from the foundation to the roof soffit. Because of the extreme weight of full-wall veneer, extensive reinforcement is required. Installation is not generally recommended for do-it-your-selfers; consult a professional.

Stucco is a durable finish that can be tinted to blend with surroundings. Window trim is removed to apply stucco to house walls. Narrow trowel cuts under the trim serve as control joints, preventing large cracks from appearing later.

Find the square footage of veneer stone required for your project by multiplying the length by the height of the area. Subtract the square footage of window and door openings and corner pieces. One linear foot of corner pieces covers approximately ¾ of a square foot of flat area, so you can reduce the square footage of flat stone required by ¾ sq. ft. for each linear foot of inside or outside corner. It's best to increase your estimate by 5 to 10 percent to allow for trimming.

Finishing Walls with Stone Veneer

If you want the look of stone on your house without the rigors of cutting and moving heavy materials, veneer stone is ideal. Two types of veneer are available. One is natural stone that has been cut into thin pieces designed for finishing walls, hearths, and other surfaces. The other is made from concrete that is molded and tinted to look like natural stone, but is even lighter and easier to apply to these surfaces.

Whether you use natural or manufactured veneer, wet each stone, then apply mortar to the back before pressing it onto the mortared wall. Wetting and mortaring a stone (called *parging*) results in maximum adhesion between the stone and the wall. The challenge is to arrange the stones so that large and small stones and various hues and shapes alternate across the span of the wall.

This project is designed for installing veneer stone over plywood sheathing, which has the strength to support layers of building paper, lath, and veneer. If your walls are covered with

fiberboard or any other type of sheathing, ask the veneer manufacturer for recommendations.

NOTE: Installing from the top down makes cleanup easier, since it reduces the amount of splatter on preceding courses. However, manufacturers advise bottom-up installation for some veneers. Read the manufacturer's guidelines carefully before you begin.

Everything You Need:

Tools: Hammer or staple gun, drill, wheelbarrow, mortar, hoe, square-end trowel, circular saw, wide-mouth nippers or mason's hammer, dust mask, level, jointing tool, mortar bag, spray bottle, whisk broom.

Materials: Type M mortar mix, mortar tint (optional), 15-lb. building paper, expanded galvanized metal lath (diamond mesh, minimum 2.5-lb.), 1½" (minimum) galvanized roofing nails or heavy-duty staples, 2 × 4 lumber

How to Finish Walls with Stone Veneer

1 Cover the wall with sheets of building paper, overlapped by 4". Nail or staple lath every 6" into the wall studs and midway between studs. Nails or staples should penetrate 1" into the studs. Paper and lath must extend at least 16" around corners where veneer is installed.

2 Stake a level 2 × 4 against the foundation as a temporary shelf to keep the bottom edge of the veneer 4" above grade. The gap between the bottom course and the ground will reduce staining of the veneer by plants and soil.

3 Spread out materials on the ground so you can select pieces of varying size, shape, and color, and create contrast in the overall appearance. Alternate the use of large and small, heavily textured and smooth, and thick and thin pieces.

4 Mix a batch of type M mortar that is firm, but still moist. Mortar that is too dry or too wet is hard to work with and may fail to bond properly.

(continued on next page)

5 Use a square-end trowel to press a ½" to ¾" layer of mortar into the lath. To ensure that mortar doesn't set up too quickly, start with a 5 sq. ft. area. Once you determine your pace, you can mortar larger areas. NOTE: You can mix in small amounts of water to retemper mortar that has begun to thicken.

6 Install corner pieces first, alternating long and short *legs*. Wet and parge (page 110) each piece, then press it firmly against the freshly mortared wall so some mortar squeezes out. Joints between stones should be no wider than ½" and should remain as consistent as possible across the wall.

7 Once the corner pieces are in place, install flat pieces, working toward the center of the wall.

8 If mortar becomes smeared on a stone, remove it with a whisk broom or soft-bristle brush after the mortar has begun to dry. Never use a wire brush or a wet brush of any kind.

9 Trim natural stone using standard stone-cutting techniques (pages 46 to 49). To cut manufactured stone, use wide-mouth nippers or a mason's hammer to trim and shape pieces to fit. Do your best to limit trimming so that each piece retains its natural look.

10 You can hide cut edges that are well above or below eye level simply by rotating a stone. If an edge remains visible, use mortar to cover. Let the mortar cure for 24 hours, then remove the 2 × 4 and stakes, taking care not to dislodge any stones.

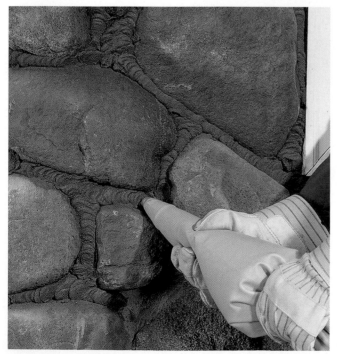

11 Fill in the joints, using a mortar bag and tuck-pointing mortar, once the wall is covered in veneer, but take extra care to avoid smearing the mortar. You can tint the tuck-pointing mortar to complement the veneer.

12 Smooth the joints with a jointing tool once the mortar is firm. Once the mortar is dry to the touch, use a dry whisk broom to remove loose mortar—water or chemicals can leave a permanent stain.

Finishing Walls with Stucco

Refinishing an entire house with stucco is a demanding job not well suited to even the most committed homeowner. It's a job best left to a stucco mason, who can complete most stucco projects in less than a week. But finishing the walls of a small addition, garage, or shed can be quite satisfying. You can use stucco to match existing walls or to create a texture that complements stone, cedar shakes, or other types of siding.

Good wall preparation is the first step for an attractive, durable finish. If the walls are wood, attach building paper and metal lath to create a tight seal and a gripping surface for the stucco. Concrete block walls are already fairly watertight and are rough enough that stucco can be applied directly to the block. During new block construction, make the mortar joints flush with the blocks in preparation for a stucco finish.

Once you've prepared the wall surface, plan to spend several days applying the three stucco coats—scratch coat, brown coat, and finish coat—that guarantee a tight seal and a professional appearance.

If the original walls of your house are finished with stucco, you'll probably need to tint your finish coat to match. Even if the stucco originally applied to your house was white, that finish has probably darkened considerably. Tinting is the best way to match the new with the old. Follow the manufacturer's instructions for the tint you purchase, and plan to experiment until you find a good match. Let each test batch dry thoroughly before you settle on the proportions. Keep notes as you test so you can reproduce the results for each subsequent batch of stucco.

By adding tint to the mixture, you can produce just about any color stucco you desire, from a subtle off-white to a stately blue.

Everything You Need:

Tools: Cement mixer, wheelbarrow, mortar hawk, mason's trowel, square-end trowel, darby or long wood float, hammer, staple gun, level, utility knife, aviation snips, spade, bucket, fine-tined metal rake.

Materials: Building paper, expanded galvanized metal lath (diamond mesh, minimum 2.5 lb.), 1½" galvanized nails, 1½" wire nails, staples, stucco mix, 1 × 2.

How to Finish a Wall with Stucco

1 Prepare the wall by attaching building paper, metal lath, and edging. Staple the building paper to the entire wall, and trim the excess with a utility knife. Trim the lath and edging to size, using aviation snips, and nail them to the wall. Rub your hand down the lath; it will feel rough when it is positioned upright. Check the edging for level.

2 Mix the scratch coat, adding water and kneading it with a trowel until it forms a workable paste. Beginning at either the top or the bottom of the wall, hold the mortar hawk close to the wall and press mud into the mesh with a square-end trowel. Press firmly to fill any voids, and cover the mesh completely.

3 Wait for the scratch coat to harden enough so that an impression remains when you press on the stucco. Rough up the surface by making shallow horizontal scratches the length of the wall. You can make a scratching tool by pounding a row of 1½" wire nails through a 1 × 2.

4 Mist the surface occasionally for 48 hours. Mix and apply the brown coat approximately ⅜" thick, then level the entire surface with a wood darby to provide a roughened gripping surface for the finish coat.

5 Mix the finish coat, adding tint as required, and slightly more water than in previous coats. The mix should still sit on the mortar hawk without running. Apply the finish coat so the edging is fully embedded (approximately ⅛" thick).

6 Finish the surface by throwing stucco at the wall with a whisk broom, then flattening the stucco with a trowel. Wait 24 hours for the finish coat to set up, then mist 2 to 3 times a day for two days, and once a day for another three days.

Building Landscape Accents

Masonry materials are ideal for creating and installing outdoor accents—from planters to barbecues—that are functional and attractive. Masonry lasts a long time, is easy to maintain, and, as this book has demonstrated, can be fashioned in a myriad of ways to blend with its surroundings. Because of the range of masonry materials, you can build small accent pieces and larger structures to complement just about any landscape.

Half the challenge—and half the enjoyment—of creating masonry accents is in the design stage. Since each piece is presumably intended for a specific location, spend some time thinking about the other elements in that area. The list includes everything from grass, gardens, and paths to

driveways, garages and the permanent structure of your house. Step back from the designated area and view it from several angles to get a clear sense of how your accent piece will fit in.

Bear in mind some practical considerations that will affect your landscape accent as well. Shade, prevailing winds, and ground moisture can all play a role in how much use an accent piece gets. A birdbath may be ideal for a wet low-lying area that is easily seen but seldom used for other purposes. A barbecue, on the other hand, belongs in a dry, comfortable spot, where you can entertain guests and have easy access to the kitchen.

Flower planters can be moveable units that stand alone or permanent structures that attached to walls, patios, or landings. Isolation boards separate this planter from the adjacent wall and landing to allow each structure to shift independently during freezing and thawing.

A driveway marker, should be proportional to the driveway and use materials that complement its surroundings. The design of a masonry project should always take into account the scale of nearby landscape elements.

A brick barbeque should be positioned near the kitchen and where there is space for guest to gather. Take into account the prevailing winds to avoid a smoke-out of your guests or your house.

Building a Stone Driveway Marker

Building a stone pillar is much like constructing a stone wall, with the added challenge of building four cornerstones into each small course. You'll need to choose your stones carefully, and remember to save a large, flat stone for a capstone. Or, buy a custom-cut stone or concrete cap to finish the top of the marker.

We built our pillar with rubble stone, which requires a lot of mortar because of the stones' irregular shapes. For strength and appearance, try to keep the mortar joints within ½" of one another in thickness. Where a thicker joint is unavoidable, you can dress it up by setting small pieces of stone into the tuck-pointing mortar during the finishing steps of the project. Review the techniques for working with stone (pages 42 to 51) before starting your project.

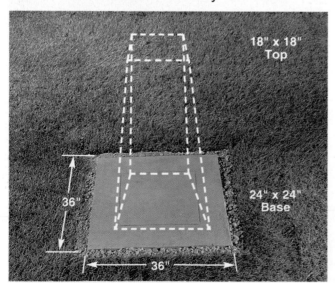

Stout dimensions and the choice of rubble stone for this driveway marker give it a rustic look. For a more stately or refined marker, use an ashlar, or trimmed stone and a more formal design.

How to Build a Stone Driveway Marker

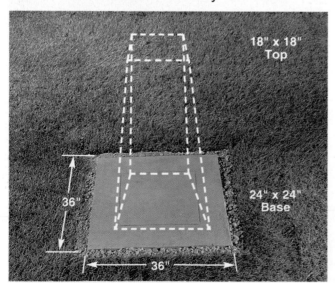

18" x 18" Top

36"

24" x 24" Base

36"

1 Pour a concrete footing that extends 6" beyond the base of the pillar on all sides (pages 38 to 41). Use the planned height of the pillar and the batter rate to calculate the size of the footing. Let the footing cure for one week.

2 Sort individual stones by size and shape. Set aside suitable tie stones for use as corner stones. Use the largest stones near the bottom. Dry-lay the outside stones in the first course to get a sense of how the stones will fit together.

3 Trowel a 1"-thick bed of mortar on the footing, then lay the stones for the first course. When the outer stones are in place, fill in the center with small stones and mortar, leaving the center slightly lower than the outer stones.

4 Pack mortar between the outer stones, recessing the mortar an equal amount, roughly 1" from the faces of the stones.

5 Set each course of stone in a bed of mortar laid over the preceding course. Stagger the vertical joints, and use a batter gauge to check slope. Place tie stones that extend into the pillar center. Use wood shims to support large stones until the mortar sets.

6 When the mortar has set enough to resist light finger pressure, smooth the joints, using a jointing tool. Keep the mortar 1" back from the stone faces. Remove the shims and fill the holes. Remove dry spattered mortar with a dry, stiff-bristle brush.

7 Lay a bed of mortar and place the capstones, then smooth joints as in step 6. Tuck-point the pillar with a mortar bag and pointing trowel, as you would a stone wall. Let it set up overnight. Mist regularly for one week while the mortar cures.

Building a Barbecue

The barbecue design shown here is constructed with double walls—an inner wall, made of heat-resistant fire brick set on edge, surrounding the cooking area, and an outer wall, made of engineer brick. We chose this brick because its stout dimensions mean you'll have fewer bricks to lay. You'll need to adjust the design if you select another brick size. A 4" air space between the walls helps insulate the cooking area. The walls are capped with thin pieces of cut stone.

Refractory mortar (page 17) is recommended for use with fire brick. It is heat resistant and the joints will last a long time without cracking. Ask a local brick yard to recommend a refractory mortar for outdoor use.

The foundation combines a 12"-deep footing supporting a reinforced slab. This structure, known as a floating footing, is designed to shift as a unit when temperature changes cause the ground to shift. Ask a building inspector about local Building Code specifications.

Everything You Need:

Tools: Tape measure, hammer, brickset chisel, mason's string, shovel, aviation snips, reciprocating saw or hack saw, line level, masonry hoe, wood float, chalk line, level, wheelbarrow, mason's trowel, jointing tool.

Materials: Garden stakes, 2 × 4 lumber, 18-gauge galvanized metal mesh, #4 rebar, 16-gauge tie wire, bolsters, fire brick (4½ × 2½ × 9"), engineer brick (4 × 3⅕ × 8"), type N mortar, refractory mortar, ⅜"-dia. dowel, metal ties, 4" tee plates, capstones (4 × 2 × 12"), brick sealer, stainless steel expanded mesh (23¾ × 30"), cooking grills (23⅝ × 15½"), ash pan.

A note about bricks: The brick sizes recommended above allow you to build the barbecue without splitting a lot of bricks. If the bricks recommended here are not easy to find in your area, a local brick yard can help you adjust the project dimensions to accommodate different brick sizes.

How to Pour a Floating Footing

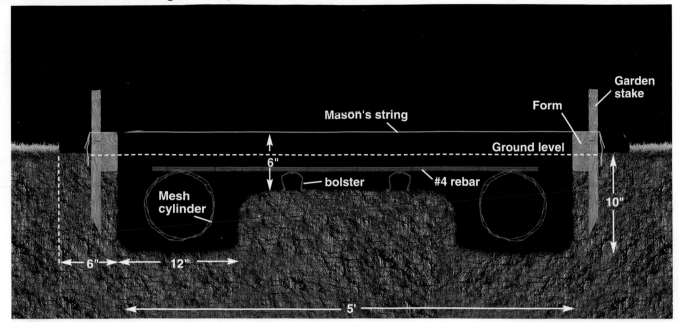

Lay out a 4 × 5 ft. area. Dig a continuous trench, 12" wide × 10" deep, along the perimeter of the area, leaving a rectangular mound in the center. Remove 4" of soil from the top of the mound, and round over the edges. Set a 2 × 4 form (page 26 to 27) around the site so that the top is 2" above the ground along the back and 1½" above the ground along the front. This slope will help shed water. Reinforce the footing with metal mesh and five 52"-long pieces of rebar. Use a mason's string and a line level to ensure that the forms

are level from side to side. Roll the mesh into 6"-dia. cylinders and cut them to fit into the trench, leaving a 4" gap between the cylinder ends and the trench sides. Tie the rebar to the mesh so the outside pieces are 4" from the front and rear sides of the trench, centered from side to side. Space the remaining three bars evenly in between. Use bolsters where necessary to suspend the bar within the pour. Coat the forms with vegetable oil, and pour the concrete.

How to Build a Barbecue

1 After the footing has cured for one week, use a chalk line to mark the layout for the inner edge of the fire brick wall. Make a line 4" in from the front edge of the footing, and a center line perpendicular to the first line. Make a 24 × 32" rectangle that starts at the 4" line and is centered on the center line.

2 Dry-lay the first course of fire brick around the outside of the rectangle, allowing for ⅛"-thick mortar joints. NOTE: Proper placement of the inner walls is necessary so they can support the grills. Start with a full brick at the 4" line to start the right and left walls. Complete the course with a cut brick in the middle of the short wall.

(continued next page)

3 Dry-lay the outer wall, as shown here, using 4 × 3⅕ × 8" nominal engineer brick. Gap the bricks for ⅜" mortar joints. The rear wall should come within ⅜" of the last fire brick in the left inner wall. Complete the left wall with a cut brick in the middle of the wall. Mark reference lines for this outer wall.

4 Make a story pole. On one side, mark eight courses of fire brick, leaving a ⅜" gap for the bottom mortar joint and ⅛" gaps for the remaining joints. The top of the final course should be 36" from the bottom edge. Transfer the top line to the other side of the pole. Lay out 11 courses of engineer brick, spacing them evenly so that the final course is flush with the 36" line. Each horizontal mortar joint will be slightly less than ½" thick.

5 Lay a bed of refractory mortar for a ⅜" joint along the reference lines for the inner wall, then lay the first course of fire brick, using ⅛" joints between the bricks.

6 Lay the first course of the outer wall, using type N mortar. Use oiled ⅜" dowels to create weep holes behind the front bricks of the left and right walls. Alternate laying the inner and outer walls, checking your work with the story pole and a level after every other course.

7 Start the second course of the outer wall using a half brick butted against each side of the inner wall, then complete the course. Because there is a half brick in the right outer wall, you need to use two three-quarter bricks in the second course to stagger the joints.

8 Place metal ties between the corners of the inner and outer walls, at the second, third, fifth, and seventh courses. Use ties at the front junctions and along the rear walls. Mortar the joint where the left inner wall meets the rear outer wall.

9 Smooth the mortar joints with a jointing tool when the mortar has hardened enough to resist minimal finger pressure. Check the joints in both walls after every few courses. The different mortars may need smoothing at different times.

10 Add tee plates for grill supports above the fifth, sixth, and seventh courses. Use 4"-wide plates with flanges that are no more than ³⁄₃₂" thick. Position the plates along the side fire brick walls, centered 3", 12", 18", and 27" from the rear fire brick wall.

11 When both walls are complete, install the capstones. Lay a bed of type N mortar for a ³⁄₈"-thick joint on top of the inner and outer walls. Lay the cap stone flat across the walls, keeping one end flush with the inner face of the fire brick. Make sure the bricks are level, and tool the joints when they are ready. After a week, seal the capstones and the joints between them with brick sealer and install the grills.

Converting Measurements

To Convert:	To:	Multiply by:
Inches	Millimeters	25.4
Inches	Centimeters	2.54
Feet	Meters	0.305
Yards	Meters	0.914
Square inches	Square centimeters	6.45
Square feet	Square meters	0.093
Square yards	Square meters	0.836
Cubic inches	Cubic centimeters	16.4
Cubic feet	Cubic meters	0.0283
Cubic yards	Cubic meters	0.765
Ounces	Milliliters	30.0
Pints (U.S.)	Liters	0.473 (Imp. 0.568)
Quarts (U.S.)	Liters	0.946 (Imp. 1.136)
Gallons (U.S.)	Liters	3.785 (Imp. 4.546)
Ounces	Grams	28.4
Pounds	Kilograms	0.454

To Convert:	To:	Multiply by:
Millimeters	Inches	0.039
Centimeters	Inches	0.394
Meters	Feet	3.28
Meters	Yards	1.09
Square centimeters	Square inches	0.155
Square meters	Square feet	10.8
Square meters	Square yards	1.2
Cubic centimeters	Cubic inches	0.061
Cubic meters	Cubic feet	35.3
Cubic meters	Cubic yards	1.31
Milliliters	Ounces	.033
Liters	Pints (U.S.)	2.114 (Imp. 1.76)
Liters	Quarts (U.S.)	1.057 (Imp. 0.88)
Liters	Gallons (U.S.)	0.264 (Imp. 0.22)
Grams	Ounces	0.035
Kilograms	Pounds	2.2

Lumber Dimensions

Nominal - U.S.	Actual - U.S.	METRIC
1 × 2	3/4 × 1 1/2"	19 × 38 mm
1 × 3	3/4 × 2 1/2"	19 × 64 mm
1 × 4	3/4 × 3 1/2"	19 × 89 mm
1 × 5	3/4 × 4 1/2"	19 × 114 mm
1 × 6	3/4 × 5 1/2"	19 × 140 mm
1 × 7	3/4 × 6 1/4"	19 × 159 mm
1 × 8	3/4 × 7 1/4"	19 × 184 mm
1 × 10	3/4 × 9 1/4"	19 × 235 mm
1 × 12	3/4 × 11 1/4"	19 × 286 mm
1 1/4 × 4	1 × 3 1/2"	25 × 89 mm
1 1/4 × 6	1 × 5 1/2"	25 × 140 mm
1 1/4 × 8	1 × 7 1/4"	25 × 184 mm
1 1/4 × 10	1 × 9 1/4"	25 × 235 mm
1 1/4 × 12	1 × 11 1/4"	25 × 286 mm
1 1/2 × 4	1 1/4 × 3 1/2"	32 × 89 mm
1 1/2 × 6	1 1/4 × 5 1/2"	32 × 140 mm
1 1/2 × 8	1 1/4 × 7 1/4"	32 × 184 mm
1 1/2 × 10	1 1/4 × 9 1/4"	32 × 235 mm
1 1/2 × 12	1 1/4 × 11 1/4"	32 × 286 mm
2 × 4	1 1/2 × 3 1/2"	38 × 89 mm
2 × 6	1 1/2 × 5 1/2"	38 × 140 mm
2 × 8	1 1/2 × 7 1/4"	38 × 184 mm
2 × 10	1 1/2 × 9 1/4"	38 × 235 mm
2 × 12	1 1/2 × 11 1/4"	38 × 286 mm
3 × 6	2 1/2 × 5 1/2"	64 × 140 mm
4 × 4	3 1/2 × 3 1/2"	89 × 89 mm
4 × 6	3 1/2 × 5 1/2"	89 × 140 mm

Liquid Measurement Equivalents

1 Pint	= 16 Fluid Ounces	= 2 Cups
1 Quart	= 32 Fluid Ounces	= 2 Pints
1 Gallon	= 128 Fluid Ounces	= 4 Quarts

Converting Temperatures

Convert degrees Fahrenheit (F) to degrees Celsius (C) by following this simple formula: Subtract 32 from the Fahrenheit temperature reading. Then, multiply that number by 5/9. For example, 77°F - 32 = 45. 45 × 5/9 = 25°C.

To convert degrees Celsius to degrees Fahrenheit, multiply the Celsius temperature reading by 9/5. Then, add 32. For example, 25°C × 9/5 = 45. 45 + 32 = 77°F.

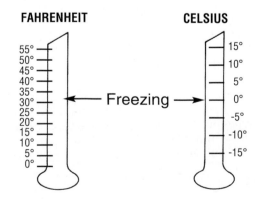

Contributors

Anchor Fence of Minnesota
7709 Pillsbury Avenue South
Richfield, MN 55423
(612) 866-4961

Buechel Stone Corp.
W3639 Hwy. H
Chilton, WI 53014-9643 ·
(800) 236-4473
www.buechelstone.com

Creative Habitats Inc.
4467 Clover Lane
Eagan, MN 55122
(651) 681-9547

Cultured Stone Corporation
P.O. Box 270
Napa, CA 94559-0270
(800) 255-1727
www.culturedstone.com

Hedberg Aggregates
1205 Nathan Lane North
Plymouth, MN 55441
(612) 545-4400
www.shadeslanding.com/
hedberg/

Interlock Concrete Products Inc.
3535 Bluff Dr.
Jordan, MN 55352-8302
(800) 780-7212
www.interlock-concrete.com

International Masonry Institute
275 Market St # 511
Minneapolis, MN 55405
(800) 464-0988
www.imiweb.org

Pittsburgh Corning Corporation
800 Presque Isle Drive
Pittsburgh, PA 15239
(800) 624-2120
www.pittsburghcorning.com

The Quikrete Companies
2987 Clairmont Rd.
Suite 500
Atlanta, GA 30329
(800) 282-5828
www.quikrete.com

Warner Manufacturing Company
13435 Industrial Park Blvd.
Minneapolis, MN 55441
(800) 444-0606
www.warnertool.com

Other Resources

Brick Institute of America
11490 Commerce Park Drive,
Suite 300
Reston, VA 20191
(703) 620-0010
www.brickinfo.org

National Concrete
Masonry Association
P.O. Box 781
2302 Horse Pen Road
Herndon, VA 20171
(703) 713-1900
www.ncma.org

Portland Cement Association
5420 Old Orchard Road
Skokie, IL 60077
(847) 966-6200
www.portcement.org

*Licensing information for brick pavers shown on page 64: UNI-Decor is a registered trademark of F. von Langsdorff Licensing Ltd., Toronto, Ontario. Symetry is a registered trademark of Symrah Licensing Incorporated, Cincinnati, Ohio.

Photo Credits

Crandall & Crandall
Dana Point, CA
© Crandall & Crandall – p. 138

Charles Mann
Santa Fe, NM
© Charles Mann – p. 91a

Jerry Pavia
Bonner's Ferry, ID
© Jerry Pavia – pp. 8a, 100a, 116,
139a, 139b

Michael S. Thompson
Eugene, OR
© Michael S. Thompson – p. 139c

INDEX